LUCA DI MARIA

Mind Over Money

Simplified Path to Financial Independence and Money Mastery

Copyright © 2024 by Luca Di Maria

All rights reserved. No part of this publication may be reproduced, stored or transmitted in any form or by any means, electronic, mechanical, photocopying, recording, scanning, or otherwise without written permission from the publisher. It is illegal to copy this book, post it to a website, or distribute it by any other means without permission.

First edition

This book was professionally typeset on Reedsy. Find out more at reedsy.com

Contents

1	Introduction	1
2	Starting Point	5
	Financial Beliefs	6
	Emotional Spending	8
	Clarifying Your Values	11
	Financial Snapshot	13
3	Defining Your Financial Freedom	25
	Importance of Enough	28
	Visualizing Milestones	30
	Aligned Aspirations	34
4	Game Plan	39
	Monthly Budget	40
	Money Leaks	43
	Emergency Fund	45
	Saving is Your Super Power	47
	Investing in Yourself First	49
	Compound Effect	51
	ETFs vs Individual Stocks	54
	Launch Your Path	57
5	Investing Beyond Money	71
	Start With Happiness Now	72
	Sustaining Financial Freedom	79
6	The Power of Structure: Designing Your Day	83
	Morning: Start Your Day Right	83

	Afternoon: Keep Momentum	85
	Evening: Reflect & Grow	88
	Staying Consistent and Focused	90
	Keep Going	93
7	Passing on Financial Wisdom	97
	Teaching Family	97
	Giving Back	99
8	Conclusion	103
9	Resources	105

1

Introduction

No alarms controlling your day, no bosses dictating your schedule. You work if you want to, travel when you choose, and spend time on what truly matters. Money isn't a source of stress — it's a tool that works for you. This is financial freedom. Not a distant dream, but a reality within reach for anyone willing to pursue it. It's not reserved for a select few; it's a right we all have. Every choice, every moment, every day is yours to design.

Financial freedom gives you options—the ability to design a life that reflects your deepest values and aspirations. It means no longer feeling trapped in a job or stuck in a cycle of living paycheck to paycheck. Instead, you gain the flexibility to pursue what matters to you. Maybe it's traveling the world, immersing yourself in different cultures, and collecting unforgettable experiences. Perhaps it's finally diving into a passion project quietly calling you for years. Or maybe it's simply being present for your loved ones—truly present, without the distractions or weight of financial stress.

But financial freedom is not just about what you gain; it's about what you overcome. It's about knowing that if life throws a curveball—whether it's an unexpected expense or an opportunity you can't pass up—you have the resources and resilience to handle it. And perhaps the most precious gift it offers is time. Time to focus on joy, growth, and fulfillment instead of constantly worrying about bills or the next paycheck. Time to live intentionally, guided by your values rather than circumstances.

When I started this journey, I didn't have a roadmap, and honestly, I didn't even think financial freedom was possible for someone like me. My parents worked hard their entire lives but were never truly free of financial worries. I followed in their footsteps, working hard, paying the bills, and repeating the cycle month after month. It felt like that was just how life worked.

One evening, I had the chance to reconnect with an old friend I hadn't seen in years, and we decided to catch up over dinner. As we chatted, he told me about his travels—how he had spent months exploring different corners of the world, immersing himself in new cultures, and living life completely on his terms. What stood out to me was how he was able to sustain that lifestyle. That conversation, which happened six years ago, turned out to be a life-changing moment for me.

That dinner sparked something deep within me. Listening to his incredible journey, I felt as though the doors to a much wider world had just swung open. I couldn't stop thinking about how he made it work, how he built a life that wasn't just about a paycheck, but about creating income streams that didn't require constant effort. What else could I do to create a life that wasn't just about earning a paycheck, but also building additional streams of income that required little to no ongoing effort?

That's when the idea of a financially free mindset began to take root in my mind. I started to realize that there were more ways to live and earn than what I had been taught. Financial freedom didn't feel like some far-off dream anymore—it became a tangible goal, something I could work toward with intention. Every day, I find myself asking, "How can I refine this? How can I create even more freedom and fulfillment?"

I hope this story resonates with you. The point of this book is to help you see the possibilities outside of the typical work routine, to show you that true happiness and freedom are within your reach. And when you get there, I hope you'll share what you've learned with others—help them find their path, just like I'm hoping to help you. If we all do this, imagine the positive ripple effect we could create—starting with you. Picture the chain reaction this could set in motion. One person at a time, the impact grows—your story inspiring theirs, their story inspiring someone else, and so on.

This book is your guide to achieving true financial freedom, step by step. It starts with understanding your current relationship with money — your beliefs, values, and financial reality. Once you have clarity on where you stand, the next step is defining where you want to be financially. With your goal in mind, you'll learn about the essential tools and strategies to build wealth, from smart investments to leveraging the power of compounding. Finally, the journey doesn't stop at wealth-building — it's about sustaining that freedom and thinking beyond money, focusing on fulfillment, purpose, and the legacy you leave behind. This book isn't just about numbers; it's about transforming your life.

Let's start the journey.

2

Starting Point

The journey to financial independence begins with a deep understanding of yourself. Before you jump into strategies, before you set those big, bold goals, it is crucial to take a moment and reflect on your relationship with money. How do you feel about it? How do you earn it, spend it, and save it? Even the way you worry about money says a lot about your underlying beliefs and values. These are the habits and thought patterns that have been shaped over time, and they are the foundation of everything that follows.

You see, understanding where you stand—not just financially, but emotionally—is the key to unlocking your true potential. Without that clarity, it's all too easy to set goals that don't align with what matters to you. You might chase numbers or milestones without understanding what will bring you fulfillment or real freedom. But when you truly get to know yourself, when you understand the deeper reasons behind your financial decisions, everything shifts.

Suddenly, every choice you make feels more intentional and more aligned with who you are and what you want in life. Each step forward isn't just a move toward more money—it's a step toward more meaning, more joy, and more peace of mind. This is where the magic happens. This is where you start to build a life that's not just about achieving financial independence, but about living with purpose and fulfillment every single day.

So, before you dive into the how-to's, take a moment to check in with yourself. Reflect on your values, your fears, and your dreams. Once you have that clarity, you'll find that every financial decision you make feels more powerful, more meaningful—and ultimately, more impactful.

Financial Beliefs

Every journey begins with a first step, and when it comes to reaching financial freedom, that first step is understanding where you're starting from. It's about taking a closer look at how you think about money, the beliefs you've picked up over the years, and how your upbringing might have shaped your habits. Think of this as the foundation for everything else. Before you can build a solid plan, you need to know where you stand.

Let's start with your mindset. How you think about money affects every financial decision you make. Some people see money as something scarce—there's never enough, and they need to hold on to what they have tightly. This mindset often leads to feeling stuck, avoiding risks, and being afraid of making mistakes. Others have an abundance mindset—they see money as a tool, something that can grow and create opportunities if used wisely. They feel more confident and are willing to take measured risks that could lead to big rewards. Take a moment to think about where you fall. Do you make decisions out of fear or out of opportunity? Don't worry if you realize your mindset leans more toward scarcity. The good news is that mindsets can change. By shifting how you think—focusing on the possibilities instead of the limits—you can start building a healthier, more confident relationship with money.

Your beliefs about money also play a huge role in shaping your mindset. Think about the messages you've picked up over the years—things like "Investing is too risky," "I'm not good with money," or "I'll never earn enough to save." These beliefs often come from what we've seen or heard growing up, especially from parents or grandparents who lived in a different financial world. While these ideas may have made sense in their time, they might not be as helpful today. Recognizing and challenging these beliefs is a big part of the work.

Finally, it's important to think about how your family and background have influenced your financial habits. Our parents and grandparents grew up in a different world with different opportunities. For example, they might have focused more on saving because they didn't have access to the financial tools we have today, like investing apps or online education. They might have seen debt as something to avoid at all costs, or they might have believed that growing wealth was only for the very rich. While these lessons were valuable for their time, today's world works differently. There are more opportunities to grow your money, whether it's through smart investments, passive income streams, or just learning better ways to manage your finances. That doesn't mean you should ignore the wisdom they passed down, like living within your means or avoiding unnecessary risks. Instead, you can combine those lessons with the tools and options available now to create your unique approach.

Taking a good, honest look at how you think about money, the beliefs you've carried, and the habits you've picked up might feel like a lot at first. But this process isn't about judgment—it's about clarity. When you understand where you are, you'll feel more prepared and confident about where you're going. Every small step you take from here will be a step in the right direction.

Understanding your mindset, beliefs, and background is the foundation of your financial journey. This process isn't about judgment—it's about awareness. When you know where you're starting, you can chart a clearer path forward. It's not about being perfect; it's about making progress, one step at a time.

Emotional Spending

Money isn't just about numbers—it's also about emotions. Every time you spend, there's usually a feeling behind it. Maybe you've bought something to cheer yourself up after a hard day or treated yourself to something fancy because you felt like you deserved it. That's emotional spending, and it happens to everyone. The key to gaining control over it isn't about stopping yourself from enjoying life; it's about spending in ways that truly make you happy and avoiding spending that doesn't.

The first step is to recognize your triggers for emotional spending. Stress is a common one. When life feels overwhelming, a shopping spree, takeout meal, or little indulgence can feel like a quick fix. Boredom is another—how often have you scrolled through online stores just to pass the time? Even happiness can lead to overspending, like splurging to celebrate a win or reward yourself. None of these are wrong, but they can lead to spending on things that don't bring lasting joy. Start noticing your patterns. When are you most likely to spend emotionally? Is it after a bad day, or when you're feeling restless? This awareness is the first step to taking back control.

Next, it's important to differentiate what makes you happy from what's just a quick emotional fix. This is where you get to be honest with yourself. Think about what truly brings value to your life. For example, if you love going to the movies once a week, that might be something worth keeping. It adds joy and meaning to your life. But if you're spending money on things that don't matter as much—like clothes you rarely wear, gadgets you don't use, or things you bought because they were on sale—those are the habits to rethink. The goal isn't to cut out what you love but to focus your spending on what brings you genuine happiness.

Your past habits also play a big role in how you spend now. Many of us grew up with certain messages about money that shaped our behaviors. Maybe you learned that buying things was a way to feel successful, or perhaps shopping was a way to bond with friends or family. These patterns can stick with you, even if they're not serving you anymore. Take some time to reflect on why you spend the way you do. What emotions or memories are behind your decisions? By understanding your habits, you can start making choices that better align with your goals.

Once you've identified your triggers and what truly makes you happy, it's time to create a plan to manage emotional spending. Start by pausing before making a purchase. Ask yourself, "Do I want this? Will it bring me lasting happiness, or is this just an emotional reaction?" Sometimes, just taking a moment to reflect can stop unnecessary spending.

Another helpful strategy is to replace emotional spending with other activities that give you the same feeling. If you're stressed, instead of shopping, try taking a walk, calling a friend, or journaling. If you're bored, dive into a hobby you love or explore something new. By finding other ways to cope with emotions, you can reduce the urge to spend without feeling deprived.

It's also useful to set boundaries for yourself. Create a "fun money" budget—a set amount you can spend guilt-free on the things that make you happy, like movie nights or dining out. This keeps your spending intentional while still letting you enjoy life. At the same time, try to cut back on unnecessary expenses, like impulse buys or things you don't use. It's not about restricting yourself—it's about putting your money where it matters most.

Remember, emotional spending doesn't make you bad with money—it just makes you human. The goal isn't to eliminate all emotional spending but to shift it toward what truly adds value to your life. By recognizing your triggers, focusing on what makes you genuinely happy, and creating mindful spending habits, you can take control of your money and feel more confident in how you use it. This balance is what brings you closer to financial freedom, one thoughtful choice at a time.

Clarifying Your Values

The first step to achieving financial independence is defining what it really means to you. Take a moment to think about your version of financial freedom. For some, it's having the ability to quit a job that drains them and pursue something they're passionate about. For others, it's about building a financial cushion that provides peace of mind in case of unexpected challenges. Financial independence isn't the same for everyone, and that's okay. What's important is that you get clear on what it looks like for you.

For me, personal freedom is all about using money as a tool to create a life that truly aligns with our values. It means having the freedom to travel with my family at least three times a year, without worrying about the cost. But more than that, it's having a passive income stream that provides the security we need, covering not just our everyday expenses, but also future needs—like our kids' education and other important milestones. This steady income gives us peace of mind, knowing we're taken care of now and in the years to come.

It also means that I can focus on doing work that I'm passionate about—projects that I truly love and that allow me to make a positive impact on others. This vision of financial independence shapes the choices I make every day, keeping me grounded in what matters most to me. It's about building a life that brings us joy, security, and the freedom to live fully, knowing that we're supporting the future we want for our family.

Once you know what financial independence means, it becomes easier to make decisions that move you closer to that goal. Ask yourself: What do I truly want in my life, and what does it take to get there? For example, if your goal is to travel more or start a business, these priorities will guide how you spend and save. If you want to retire early, you'll need to focus on building long-term savings and investments. When you have a clear vision, you can align your actions with your financial goals.

Next, take a look at your spending habits and make sure they match your values. Often, we spend money on things that don't bring us lasting happiness, simply because they're convenient or trendy. It's important to ask yourself: Does this purchase bring me closer to my goals? If you value health, for instance, spending on a gym membership or nutritious food makes sense. But if you're spending money on things that don't align with your priorities, it's time to adjust.

Finally, differentiate between your needs and wants. Needs are things like housing, food, and healthcare—essentials for survival and well-being. Wants are the extras, like dining out, shopping, or entertainment. There's nothing wrong with spending on wants, but if your goal is financial independence, it's important to focus on the long-term picture. Start by identifying the things that truly bring you joy or add value to your life. Then, prioritize those while cutting back on unnecessary expenses. This doesn't mean eliminating fun, but it does mean being intentional with your spending.

By making clear choices about where your money goes, you're taking practical steps toward financial independence. When your spending aligns with your values and long-term goals, every dollar becomes an investment in the life you want to create.

Before moving on to the next chapters, I encourage you to take some time to think about your vision of financial freedom. This vision doesn't have to be set in stone—it can and likely will evolve as your life and goals change over time. But having a clear idea of where you want to go is essential to understanding how to get there. Having a baseline vision helps you stay focused and provides direction as you work through the next steps. So, take a moment now to reflect on what financial freedom looks like for you and why it's important. This is the foundation that will guide you through the rest of your journey.

Financial Snapshot

Before you can make real, powerful progress toward financial independence, it's important to first understand where you stand. Think of this as creating a map for your financial journey. Without it, you may wander, not knowing if you're heading in the right direction. This self-assessment is about looking closely at your current income, expenses, debts, and savings. It's about identifying where you're spending money that doesn't align with your goals and figuring out areas where you can save or invest more efficiently.

By taking the time to understand your financial situation, you'll get a clear picture of what's working well, what isn't, and where you should focus your attention next. This isn't about feeling guilty or discouraged—this is about gaining clarity on how to improve your financial situation step by step. Once you have this understanding, you'll be able to make decisions that move you closer to your financial goals.

So, let's jump in and take a close look at your financial starting point. This step is the foundation for everything that comes after. The clearer you are about where you're starting from, the more powerful your journey to financial independence will be.

Income Analysis

The first step toward financial independence is understanding where your money comes from. Take some time to list out all the sources of income you have. This might include your regular salary, any side gigs or freelance work, income from investments, or other sources like rental properties or online businesses. Write it all down—seeing everything in front of you will give you a clearer picture of your financial landscape.

It's also important to note any income that isn't consistent month-to-month. For example, if you receive an annual bonus or you earn seasonal income from a side job, make sure to account for those as well. These irregular sources of income can sometimes throw off your budgeting if you're not planning for them, so knowing how much you earn on average each month, including these fluctuations, will give you a concrete starting point.

Once you've listed all your income sources, the next step is to break your spending into two main categories: **essentials** and **discretionary**. Essentials are non-negotiable expenses like rent or mortgage, utilities, groceries, and transportation costs. These are the things you need to live day-to-day. Discretionary spending is where you have more flexibility—things like dining out, entertainment, shopping, or subscriptions to services you don't need.

Now, take a look at your essential and discretionary expenses side by side. Are there any areas where you can cut back? For example, can you reduce your grocery bill by meal planning, or cancel a subscription service you rarely use? This simple step of separating your spending will help you see where your money is going and give you a starting point for cutting back where it counts.

By getting clear on your income and spending habits, you'll have the foundation you need to create a budget that works for you. It's about knowing your numbers and making informed choices moving forward.

Here's a simple table that you can use to visualize the breakdown of income versus outcomes. It will help you get a clear picture of where your money comes from and where it goes.

Income Sources	Amount ($)	Outcome Categories	Amount ($)
Salary (Monthly)	$3,500	Essentials	
Freelance/Side Gigs	$500	Rent/Mortgage	$1,000
Investment Income	$200	Utilities (Electricity, Water)	$150
Bonus (Annual)	$1,000	Groceries	$400
Other Income (Rental, etc.)	$300	Transportation (Gas, Bus, etc.)	$200
Total Monthly Income	$5,500	Discretionary	
		Dining Out	$200
		Entertainment (Movies, etc.)	$100
		Shopping (Clothes, etc.)	$150
		Subscriptions (Netflix, etc.)	$50
Total Spending	$3,750	Total Expenses	$2,750
Savings Potential	$1,750		

This table helps you visualize where your income is coming from and how your expenses break down. The goal is to look at your spending and find areas where you can adjust. Maybe you can cut back on discretionary spending like dining out or shopping, and funnel that money into savings or investing.

By tracking income and outcomes, you'll have a clear understanding of your financial flow, allowing you to make smarter, more intentional decisions about where to allocate your resources

I keep a similar format in my Google Sheets online, which I can access anytime from my phone or laptop. It's incredibly convenient for tracking monthly income and expenses, spotting trends, and ensuring I'm staying on track with my financial goals.

Spending Habits

For one month, commit to tracking every single expense. Yes, every single one. It might feel tedious at first, but trust me, it's one of the most eye-opening exercises you can do for your finances. This isn't just about writing numbers down; it's about creating awareness. Often, we underestimate how much we're spending in certain areas, and this process shines a light on exactly where your money is going.

As you track, categorize each expense into two groups: essential and discretionary. Essentials are the things you truly need, like rent or mortgage payments, utilities, groceries, and transportation. Discretionary expenses are everything else—dining out, subscriptions, entertainment, and those impulsive online shopping sprees.

Once you've gathered this data, it's time to dig deeper. Look for patterns or what I like to call "spending leaks." These are small, often unnoticed expenses that can add up over time. Maybe you're paying for a gym membership you barely use or have streaming subscriptions you forgot about. Perhaps your daily coffee habit is costing more than you realize. These leaks aren't inherently bad, but recognizing them gives you the power to decide if they're worth it.

Here's where the magic happens: instead of eliminating all the things that bring you joy, focus on trimming the excess—the spending that isn't adding real value to your life. For example, if your morning coffee run is a ritual you truly enjoy, keep it. But if you're ordering takeout out of convenience three times a week and not even enjoying it, that's an opportunity to save.

Let's make this practical. Start by setting a budget for your discretionary spending. This isn't about deprivation; it's about directing your money toward what matters most to you. Maybe that means cutting back on random purchases so you can save for a family vacation, invest in your future, or build your emergency fund.

To make this process easier, use a simple tool like an app, a spreadsheet, or even a notebook. I've found that tracking my spending digitally—whether in Google Sheets or with a finance app—helps me stay consistent. Plus, it's satisfying to see my progress at the end of the month.

Remember, this isn't just an exercise in discipline. It's a way to align your spending with your values and goals. By gaining control of your money in small, intentional ways, you'll free up resources to create the life you truly want—whether that's more financial security, new opportunities, or the freedom to pursue your dreams.

Understanding Liabilities and Assets

To get a clear picture of your financial situation, you need to understand two basic things: what you own and what you owe. These are called assets and liabilities. Getting a handle on these is the first step to building a solid financial foundation.

Start with What You Owe. Liabilities are the things that cost you money. This includes credit card debt, student loans, car loans, mortgages, and even overdue bills. Start by making a list of everything you owe. For each item, write down the total amount, the interest rate, and the minimum monthly payment.

When you see it all laid out, you'll understand where your money is going. Some debts, like high-interest credit cards, take a bigger bite out of your finances, while others, like a mortgage, might be more manageable. The key is to focus on the most expensive debts first—like those with high interest rates—because paying them off will free up money faster for other goals.

Next, Look at What You Own. Assets are the things that add value to your life or make you money. These can include savings accounts, investments like stocks or retirement funds, property you own, or even items you could sell for cash. Make a list of your assets, and write down their current value.

Think of your assets as tools that help you build your future. For example, your savings can act as a safety net, while investments grow over time to give you more financial freedom. Even small assets, like a side hustle that brings in extra money, can make a difference.

Finding Balance. The goal is to have more assets than liabilities over time. This won't happen overnight, and that's okay. The important thing is to start shifting the balance.

1. **Reduce What You Owe.** If you have debt with high interest, focus on paying it down as quickly as you can. Even adding a little extra to your monthly payment can make a big difference over time. If you're managing long-term debt, like a mortgage, just keep making regular payments while you work on building up your assets.
2. **Grow What You Own.** Start small. If you don't already have savings, set aside a little each month. Even $50 can add up over time. If you're new to investing, consider starting with simple options like index funds or ETFs, which spread out your risk. You can also think about learning a new skill or starting a side project to bring in extra income.

Track Your Progress. Once you've listed your assets and liabilities, subtract what you owe from what you own. This number is called your net worth. It's your starting point. Check-in on it regularly—once a month or every few months—to see how you're doing. Watching your net worth grow, even a little, can be motivating and show you that your efforts are paying off.

Why It's Important. Knowing what you own and what you owe isn't just about the numbers—it's about taking control of your money. When you see the full picture, you can make smarter decisions. Maybe you'll decide to pay off a loan faster, save for an emergency fund, or invest in something that builds wealth over time.

Every little step you take, whether it's cutting back on a small expense or putting extra cash into savings, helps move you closer to financial freedom. Over time, you're creating a system where your money works for you, so you're not always working for it. It's not about being perfect—it's about making progress and taking steps toward a better, more secure future.

Debt and Savings Review

Let's take a closer look at your debts and savings. Understanding these two areas is key to building a stronger financial future. Start by listing out every debt you owe. This could include credit card balances, student loans, car loans, personal loans, or even a mortgage. For each debt, note the total amount, the interest rate, and the minimum monthly payment. Paying attention to the interest rates is crucial because higher rates mean the debt will grow faster if left unchecked. For example, a credit card with a 20% interest rate can snowball quickly, while a car loan at 5% might be more manageable. Seeing these numbers clearly will help you prioritize which debts to tackle first.

Now, shift your focus to your savings. Begin by checking whether you have an emergency fund. This is a safety net for unexpected expenses like medical bills or car repairs. If you don't have one, aim to start saving three to six months' worth of essential living expenses. It's okay to start small—even setting aside a little each week can build up over time. After your emergency fund, take a moment to review any other savings or investments you have. Are you contributing to a retirement fund? Do you have money set aside for big goals like buying a house, starting a business, or going on a dream trip?

Once you've gathered all this information, compare your debts and savings side by side. This step might feel overwhelming, especially if your debts outweigh your savings, but it's an important reality check. Understanding where you are today allows you to make a solid plan for tomorrow.

From here, the goal is to take actionable steps. Start by focusing on the debt with the highest interest rate, as paying it down will save you the most money in the long run. Even small additional payments toward this debt each month can make a significant impact. At the same time, prioritize building your emergency fund if you don't already have one. Consider automating your savings by setting up automatic transfers to a separate account. This creates consistency and ensures that saving becomes a habit without requiring constant effort.

Throughout this process, remember to acknowledge your progress. Each debt you pay off and every bit of savings you grow is a step closer to financial freedom. This isn't just about numbers—it's about taking control of your money so it stops controlling you. By consistently working on your debts and savings, you're not only creating a more stable financial future but also gaining the confidence and clarity to pursue bigger goals.

Determining Your Net Worth

The final step in understanding your financial standing is calculating your net worth. This figure serves as your definitive benchmark, offering a clear and measurable representation of where you stand on your journey to financial freedom. Here's how to calculate it in a systematic way:

1. **Compile Your Assets**: Begin by listing all assets of value that you own. This includes cash, savings, investments (stocks, bonds, retirement accounts), real estate, vehicles, and any other valuable items such as jewelry or collectibles. Assess their current market value to ensure an accurate total.
2. **Identify Your Liabilities**: Next, list all of your liabilities. These are the debts or obligations you owe, such as mortgages, car loans, student loans, credit card balances, and any other outstanding liabilities. Be thorough in accounting for every debt, no matter how small, to gain a complete financial picture.
3. **Calculate Your Net Worth**: Subtract the total liabilities from your total assets. The result is your **net worth**—a clear indication of your financial reality. A positive net worth shows that your assets exceed your liabilities, while a negative net worth highlights areas needing attention.

Think of your net worth as your financial starting point. This number is not static; it will fluctuate over time as you build wealth and reduce debt. For that reason, it's critical to track this figure regularly—whether monthly, quarterly, or annually—so you can measure your progress and make adjustments as needed.

As you continue to build your financial future, your goal should be to increase your assets and reduce your liabilities. Each time your net worth rises, it signifies that you are moving closer to financial independence. These incremental improvements serve as concrete milestones, offering motivation and reinforcing the steps you're taking toward achieving your long-term financial goals.

By consistently evaluating key areas—your income, spending habits, assets, and liabilities—you are fortifying the foundation upon which your financial future will be built. The more precisely you understand your financial landscape, the better equipped you will be to make informed decisions that will accelerate your progress toward freedom. Every positive action you take, from reducing debt to growing your investments, compounds over time, moving you closer to the lifestyle and security you envision. This process is just the beginning. Each strategic decision, each small improvement, brings you ever closer to the life you've set out to create.

3

Defining Your Financial Freedom

Let's pause and think about what financial freedom truly means for you. Picture it in your mind: How would you spend your days if money were no longer a source of stress? Would you travel the world, start a business you're passionate about, or simply enjoy more time with your loved ones? Imagine where you'd live, your experiences, and the peace of mind that comes with knowing your finances support the life you want to live. Financial freedom is deeply personal, and taking the time to reflect on it is an important first step in defining your journey.

Ask yourself, *"Where do I want to wake up every day?"* Financial freedom gives you the power to choose your location. It could mean living by the beach, in the mountains, or staying where you are but with the flexibility to travel whenever you want. You're no longer tied to one place just because of a job.

Now think about *how you want to work*. Do you want to work 40 hours a week, 20 hours, or maybe take extended time off? Financial freedom allows you to break free from the 9-to-5 grind. You choose your schedule instead of being controlled by it.

True financial freedom is about aligning your wealth with the *life you want to live*. It's not about following someone else's plan — it's about creating your own. When you have control over your time and location, you have the freedom to live a life that feels authentically yours.

For young people, financial freedom might look like having enough passive income to travel the world, pursue passions, or start their own business without worrying about a traditional 9-to-5 job. It's about having the flexibility to design their lifestyle and live on their terms, perhaps even living in different cities or countries without the constraints of financial stress.

For those later in life, financial freedom may look like the ability to retire comfortably, knowing they have enough savings and investments to enjoy their golden years without the stress of working. It's about having the freedom to travel, pursue hobbies, and spend time with loved ones without worrying about finances. It could also mean the peace of mind that comes from knowing their family is taken care of, and they can leave a meaningful legacy behind.

Understanding the difference between financial freedom and financial security is also essential. Financial security means having enough to cover your basic needs—food, shelter, and bills. Financial freedom goes beyond that. It's about creating choices, flexibility, and opportunities. It means having the resources to live life on your terms, whether that's pursuing hobbies, taking risks like starting a new career or giving back to your community. Understanding this distinction will help you set goals that are not just about survival, but about thriving.

To make this vision tangible, write down a personal statement describing what financial freedom looks like for you. This statement should reflect your unique values and priorities. Maybe it's about paying off your mortgage, funding your kids' education, and retiring early. Or maybe it's having the means to travel frequently while still building a legacy of wealth for future generations. There's no right or wrong answer—your vision should reflect what truly matters to you.

When crafting your vision, think with the end in mind. Set a specific outcome that will signify, "I've made it." For instance, you might decide that being debt-free, having $1 million in investments, or generating enough passive income to replace your current salary is the ultimate milestone. Having this clarity is crucial because it gives you a target to work toward.

Being specific with your money goals makes them clearer and more achievable. Here are some examples:

1. **Save for an Emergency Fund**: "I will save $5,000 for my emergency fund by the end of 2024 by setting aside $250 each month."
2. **Pay off Debt**: "I will pay off my $10,000 credit card debt within 18 months by paying $555 each month, starting this month."
3. **Investing**: "I will invest $2,000 in an index fund by March 2025, contributing $100 every month until I reach that

goal."
4. **Home Purchase**: "I will save $20,000 for a down payment on a house by 2026, putting away $400 each month."
5. **Retirement Savings**: "I will increase my 401(k) contribution by 3% starting in January 2024 to ensure I save $150,000 for retirement by age 65."
6. **Building Passive Income**: "I will create a passive income stream by investing in rental properties, purchasing my first property worth $150,000 by the end of 2025."

Each of these examples is clear, measurable, and tied to a specific deadline, making it easier to track progress and stay motivated.

As you reflect on your journey, remember that your vision doesn't have to be perfect or final. Life changes, and so can your goals. But having a clear baseline gives you a direction—a sense of purpose to guide your financial decisions. Take the time to write your vision and define your end goal. This clarity will keep you motivated and ensure that your financial freedom isn't just a dream but a reality you're steadily working toward.

Importance of Enough

It's so important to find balance while working toward your financial goals. There's a lesson to learn from people who chased success so hard that they gave up other parts of their lives. Some people become so focused on making money that they push themselves too far—working all the time, neglecting their health, and letting their relationships suffer. In their race for more, they often miss out on the small, everyday moments that bring real happiness and meaning.

Look at Jordan Belfort, known as "The Wolf of Wall Street," and Bernie Madoff. Both were incredibly wealthy, but their greed led to their downfall. Belfort made millions through illegal stock deals, but it cost him his freedom, his integrity, and many of his relationships. Madoff ran a massive Ponzi scheme that brought him billions, but in the end, his lies destroyed countless lives, including his own, leaving him with nothing but regret and disgrace. These examples remind us that chasing financial success at any cost often comes with terrible consequences.

True financial freedom isn't just about having a lot of money. It's about building a life that feels full and meaningful, where your money works for you and supports the things you truly care about—your values, relationships, and passions. That's why it's so important to have a clear goal in mind. Without one, you might find yourself endlessly chasing more, never feeling like you've reached enough, and missing the chance to enjoy what you already have.

Happiness comes from knowing what you're working toward and recognizing when you've achieved it. Without a clear destination, it's easy to get lost in the constant pursuit of "more," never stopping to feel grateful or fulfilled. Take time to define what financial freedom means to you. By setting a clear vision, you'll give yourself permission to enjoy the journey, celebrate your progress, and build a life you truly love. The key isn't just to make money—it's to use it wisely to create lasting happiness and purpose.

Visualizing Milestones

Once you have a clear vision of your financial freedom, the next step is to break it down into smaller, manageable milestones. Think of these as stepping stones that lead you toward your ultimate goal. Trying to tackle everything at once can feel overwhelming, but focusing on one milestone at a time makes the journey more achievable and rewarding. For some, saving $1,000 might feel like a big challenge, but let's see how breaking it down into smaller steps can make it much more manageable.

Reaching your savings goal becomes much easier when you break it into small, manageable steps. Start by setting a simple weekly target, like saving $20—about the cost of skipping a few takeout meals or cutting back on small extras like coffee runs. Look for one expense you can temporarily reduce, such as eating out or unused subscription services. Whenever you come across extra money, like a bonus, gift, or earnings from selling items you no longer need, put it directly into your savings. To stay on track, open a separate savings account for this goal; watching your progress grow without dipping into it can be incredibly motivating.

These small steps add up quickly, and before you know it, you'll reach the $1,000 mark!

Now that you have a clear vision for your financial future and a plan with actionable steps, it's time to take things a step further to boost your chances of success. One powerful way to stay motivated is by incorporating visualization and gratitude into your daily routine. Take a few moments each day to imagine what it will feel like to reach your financial goals—whether it's being debt-free, having a secure emergency fund, or seeing your passive income cover your living expenses. Visualize that life, and let yourself feel the excitement of achieving it.

Along with this, make it a habit to write down your goals every day. This isn't just about remembering them; it's about strengthening your connection to your vision and feeling more deeply committed to it. As you write, pause for a moment to acknowledge and appreciate the progress you've already made. Even the smallest steps count, and practicing gratitude for them helps you stay positive and focused. Studies have shown that regularly visualizing your success and expressing gratitude can significantly improve your mindset, helping you stay motivated and aligned with your goals.

With each step, your vision of financial freedom will begin to feel more real. As you hit milestones, you'll build confidence and gain momentum, making the end goal feel more achievable. By staying focused, energized, and grateful for how far you've come, you'll keep moving forward with purpose, and before you know it, you'll be closer than ever to living the life you've dreamed of.

I've always been fascinated by basketball, and one story that sticks with me is a powerful study on the impact of visualization led by psychologist Alan Richardson. It beautifully illustrates just how much our minds can influence our performance. In this study, basketball players were divided into three groups. The first group practiced free throws daily, the second group didn't physically practice but visualized themselves making successful shots, and the third group did nothing at all. The results were astonishing — the players who visualized success improved nearly as much as those who practiced every day. This study is a testament to the power of the mind and how mental rehearsal can bring real-world results. It's a reminder that even when you're not "doing," you can still be progressing.

So, how does this relate to financial freedom? Just like athletes visualize success on the court, you can visualize your financial goals and train your mind to believe they're achievable. Picture yourself living debt-free, seeing your investment accounts grow, or enjoying the freedom to choose how you spend your time. This mental rehearsal strengthens your belief in your goals, keeps you focused on daily actions that support them, and reduces self-doubt. Just like the basketball players, your mind starts to believe that success is possible — and that belief drives your actions, decisions, and, ultimately, your results.

Michael Phelps, the most decorated Olympian of all time, used visualization as a cornerstone of his training. His coach, Bob Bowman, encouraged him to mentally rehearse every aspect of his races. Each night before bed, Phelps would close his eyes and visualize himself swimming his perfect race. He imagined every detail—the feel of the water, the sound of the starting gun, and even how he would overcome any obstacles, like a bad start or a disrupted rhythm. This mental practice was so vivid that when he got into the pool, it felt like he was simply replaying what he had already accomplished in his mind.

A famous moment highlighting the power of his visualization came during the 2008 Beijing Olympics. In the 200-meter butterfly final, Phelps' goggles filled with water, blinding him for most of the race. But instead of panicking, he relied on his mental rehearsals. He had visualized what to do in situations like this countless times, so he swam the race by feel and rhythm alone—and won gold, breaking the world record.

Other notable figures have also leveraged visualization. Jim Carrey, for instance, famously wrote himself a $10 million check for "acting services rendered" when he was struggling in his career. He visualized achieving his dream every day, and years later, he received exactly $10 million for his role in *Dumb and Dumber*. Oprah Winfrey, another advocate for visualization, often credits her success to her ability to see her goals clearly in her mind before making them a reality.

There is plenty more, but these examples show that visualization isn't just a way to stay motivated—it's a powerful method for reaching your goals. When you picture your goals as if you've already achieved them and imagine the steps you'll take to get there, it helps you stay focused and prepared. This process connects your thoughts to your actions, making your goals feel more real and easier to achieve.

Taking it even further, you might consider saying your goals aloud with gratitude. When you speak your goals out loud, especially with a sense of appreciation for what you've already achieved, you're not only reinforcing your commitment but also sending a powerful message to your subconscious mind. This practice helps program your brain to focus on success and keeps you aligned with your intentions. Research has shown that vocalizing your goals with gratitude can strengthen your belief in them, increase your confidence, and make it easier for you to take the necessary actions to reach them.

For example, while driving, you could say, "I'm grateful for the progress I've made towards financial freedom. I'm on track to pay off my debt and grow my savings. Every day, I'm getting closer to having a passive income that covers my expenses." Speaking this out loud helps keep you focused and aligned with your financial goals.

Try this for at least a month, and you'll see great things unfolding. Speaking your goals with sincerity and gratitude has contributed to my success in life. It shifts your mindset, boosts motivation, and keeps you focused on the actions that lead to real progress. It's a small habit that can greatly impact your financial journey and overall life success.

Aligned Aspirations

When setting financial goals, defining the kind of person you want to become is crucial. For example, instead of simply saying, "I want to save $100,000," think about who you want to be in the process of reaching that goal. You could say, "I consistently save and make wise financial decisions." This approach connects your goal to your identity, making it something you *are* rather than something you *do* occasionally.

By aligning your goals with this identity, you create intrinsic motivation. The motivation comes not from reaching a number, but from embodying the qualities of the person you want to become. When you identify as someone who is disciplined with money, your actions will naturally follow suit.

This mindset is similar to the difference between saying, "I want to reach 12% body fat," and saying, "I am an athlete who works out regularly, and maintaining my 12% body fat is non-negotiable." The first goal might give you a target to reach, but once you hit it, you might slip back into old habits. The second goal, however, becomes part of your lifestyle and identity. It's not just about reaching a destination, but about committing to daily habits that maintain the desired result.

Similarly, in your financial journey, focus on small, repeated actions that align with the identity of someone who is financially disciplined. This could mean setting aside a certain amount every week for savings or reviewing your budget every Sunday. By building systems and habits around your goals, you turn your financial success into a part of who you are—something that's consistent and sustainable, rather than a one-time achievement.

Use Tracking Tools

One of the most effective ways to build strong financial habits is to track your progress consistently. Having a visible tracker, whether it's a simple savings chart on your wall or an app on your phone, helps keep your goals front and center. By regularly monitoring your progress, you can see how small actions lead to big results over time, which reinforces the positive behaviors you're working to establish. Every time you check off a task or mark a milestone, it provides a visual reminder of your commitment to financial freedom.

Another powerful tool for making habits stick is the "two-minute rule." This rule, popularized by James Clear in *Atomic Habits*, encourages you to make your habit so simple that it takes no more than two minutes to complete. For example, you could make it a habit to briefly review your expenses each night. Instead of thinking, "I need to sit down and do a full financial audit," aim for a quick glance at your spending, perhaps using an app to track it. This small, quick check-in can become a daily habit, and over time, it keeps you aware and in control of your money without feeling overwhelmed.

Finally, use digital tools and apps to automate your financial habits. Automating your savings, bill payments, or even investments can remove the guesswork and ensure you stay on track without constant effort. Set up automatic transfers to your savings account or investment portfolio, so you're consistently moving closer to your financial goals without having to remember to take action every time. These tools serve as gentle reminders to keep you accountable and ensure your habits continue to align with your vision of financial freedom.

For me, my way of tracking progress was going to a local coffee shop, ordering my favorite flat white, and spending time reviewing my financial project. It wasn't just about looking at numbers; it was about taking a moment to reflect on how far I'd come and where I still wanted to go. This became a ritual that was not only productive but also enjoyable, reinforcing my commitment to my financial journey. It was a simple, yet powerful, habit that helped me stay motivated and aligned with my goals.

Baseline check

It's essential to regularly step back and assess whether your financial plan is still in alignment with your current circumstances. Life is constantly changing, and the path to financial freedom is rarely a straight line. There will be times when things go as planned, but there will also be moments when life throws you unexpected curveballs. These changes can come in many forms—whether it's a job promotion, an unexpected medical expense, or even just a shift in your priorities.

It's so important to take a moment now and then to check in with yourself and ask: "Is this plan still working for me?" and "Do I need to make adjustments?" It's perfectly normal for your circumstances to evolve, and what worked well six months ago may not be the best strategy today. Think of your financial goals as a living, breathing thing—something that can grow and change as you do.

For example, if you receive a raise, a bonus, or have a change in income, it might be time to review your goals and increase your savings or investment contributions. On the other hand, if you face an unexpected expense, like a car repair or a health issue, you might need to adjust your budget temporarily to accommodate that. And that's okay! It's all about being flexible and understanding that your goals aren't set in stone—they are a reflection of where you are now and where you want to go.

Remember, the key is to not become rigid with your financial plan. Life can be unpredictable, and staying open to making changes as needed allows you to stay grounded and focused on your ultimate goal of financial freedom. By consistently evaluating your circumstances and making the necessary adjustments, you ensure that you are moving forward with clarity and purpose.

Make sure the baseline you've set still reflects where you want to go and be kind to yourself if you need to make adjustments. The journey to financial freedom is about staying adaptable, staying focused, and making sure that your plan continues to align with your life as it evolves. Keep moving forward, one thoughtful decision at a time.

By now, you should have a clear vision of where you want to go. Now, let's focus on taking the essential steps to make that vision a reality.

4

Game Plan

Achieving financial freedom requires a solid game plan, and this book has laid out a clear path to follow. It starts with setting a realistic budget that puts you in control of your finances, helping you see where your money is going and where it can be better utilized. Next is building an emergency fund, a financial safety net that shields you from unexpected expenses and prevents you from falling into debt. Beyond that, we explore lesser-known saving strategies that many people overlook — from automated savings to taking advantage of compound interest and maximizing high-yield savings accounts. Each step builds on the last, forming a comprehensive strategy that not only secures your present but also sets you up for a financially free future. With this game plan in hand, you have everything you need to move from financial stress to financial confidence.

Monthly Budget

A budget is the foundation of financial freedom—it's like a roadmap that guides you toward your goals. Without it, you might find yourself wondering where your money goes each month and feeling stuck in a cycle of stress. Creating a budget puts you back in control. It helps you see the full picture of your finances, identify areas to cut back and ensure that your money is being used in ways that truly matter to you. Think of it as giving every dollar a purpose. When you know exactly where your money is going, you can start making intentional choices that bring you closer to financial independence.

Achieving financial independence starts with creating a clear, actionable plan for how you manage your money every month. One of the most effective ways to do this is by setting a budget that works for you and tracking your progress consistently. There are many budgeting methods you can choose from, but one of the most straightforward and popular methods is the 50/30/20 rule.

The 50/30/20 rule is a simple and effective way to manage your money, giving you a clear structure for how to allocate your income. To make it even more practical, consider using separate debit cards for each category. Each month, top up these cards with the set amount for their respective categories. This approach helps you track spending effortlessly—when a card runs out, it's a clear sign you've hit your limit for that category.

Here's how the rule works:

- **50% for Needs:** This is for essential expenses—things you must pay for to live, like housing, utilities, groceries, insurance, and transportation. Load half your income onto a debit card dedicated to this category to ensure your necessities are always covered.
- **30% for Wants:** This category is for the things you enjoy but don't absolutely need, like dining out, entertainment, shopping, hobbies, or vacations. Use a separate card for this spending. If the "wants" card runs dry, it's a reminder to pause and reflect that these extras can wait.
- **20% for Savings and Debt Repayment:** This portion is for building your future—saving for emergencies, investing, or paying down debt. Automate this part as much as possible so it happens without requiring additional effort.

If you and your partner are managing finances together, you might also consider having joint accounts for these categories. For instance, a shared account for "Needs" can cover rent, groceries, and other household essentials, while joint savings accounts can help you align on larger goals like buying a home or building an emergency fund. Having transparency and mutual agreement about these accounts strengthens both your financial plan and your partnership.

This system not only keeps you organized but also creates clear boundaries around spending, making it easier to stick to your budget and achieve your goals. Over time, the discipline of using separate cards or joint accounts helps you build healthier financial habits and a more secure future.

Once you get comfortable with this method and see how it

works for you, you can explore other splits or approaches that better fit your unique situation. But starting with something simple, like the 50/30/20 rule, will give you a solid understanding of where your money is going and help you take those first steps toward financial freedom.

Once you set your budget, it's crucial to track your spending regularly to ensure you're staying on track. For some, this can be done through a simple spreadsheet, while others prefer using budgeting apps that automatically track spending and categorize it for them. The key is consistency—making sure that you are actively checking your budget, and adjusting it when necessary.

To automate your savings, consider setting up automatic transfers to a separate savings account. This "pay yourself first" strategy ensures that you're always saving before you have a chance to spend the money elsewhere. For example, if you're aiming to save $500 a month, set up an automatic transfer from your checking account to your savings account as soon as your paycheck hits. This eliminates the temptation to skip savings and helps you build a solid financial foundation without thinking about it.

In addition to monthly budgeting, it's important to plan for the year ahead by allocating yearly funds into essential and non-essential categories. For example, you might set aside funds for annual expenses like property taxes or insurance premiums, as well as things like travel or large purchases you want to make. By planning for both the big and small expenses, you avoid unexpected financial surprises throughout the year.

One of the best ways to stay on top of your financial plan is to regularly review and adjust your budget. I set aside time every last Sunday of the month to dive into my financials. This is when I take a detailed look at where I've spent money and categorize each purchase into the main classes—essential needs, discretionary wants, and savings. For example, I'll review how much I spent on groceries, utilities, dining out, movies, or shopping (wants), and then compare how much I saved that month. This allows me to understand whether I'm sticking to my goals or need to make adjustments for the next month.

Money Leaks

Once you've created a budget and started saving, the next key step is to address your most painful money leaks—your debts. Tackling these financial burdens head-on is essential for regaining control over your money and making real progress toward financial freedom.

The first step in addressing your financial leaks is to identify where your money is slipping away. Start by listing all your debts—credit cards, loans, and any other outstanding balances. Make sure to note the amounts owed, interest rates, and minimum payments for each. This will give you a full picture of your financial situation and help you prioritize what needs to be tackled first.

Your highest priority should be paying off debts with the highest interest rates—typically, credit card balances. These debts can grow quickly, draining your finances with high-interest payments. By focusing on paying off your credit cards or other high-interest debts first, you'll stop the financial bleed and save more money in the long run.

Once you've paid off high-interest debts, you can think about tackling lower-interest ones—but only if paying them off is a better choice than using your money elsewhere. For example, investing in an ETF (Exchange-Traded Fund) with a potential 10% return each year could be a smarter move than paying off low-interest debt. We'll dive deeper into ETFs later in the book. The key is to consider the return on investment (ROI), which measures how much you earn from an investment compared to what you spend. ROI is important because it helps you make smarter financial decisions by showing where your money can work hardest for you. Always weigh your options and choose the one that will bring the most financial benefit. Treat it like a business decision—make sure every dollar you spend or invest works as hard as possible for you.

Once you've tackled those, you're on a much stronger path. If high-interest debts aren't a concern for you, then you're in a great position to explore other financial opportunities, like saving or investing, to grow your wealth. This is an important milestone in your financial journey. It means you've laid a solid foundation for financial stability and freedom. Being free from these high-cost burdens allows you to focus on growing your wealth and investing in your future. It's a sign of smart decision-making and discipline, and you're now in a much stronger position to move forward and explore new financial opportunities. This is a crucial step that sets you apart, so take a moment to appreciate how far you've come and treat yourself to something you've been wanting, whether it's a nice meal, a relaxing day off, or a small gift. You've earned it!

Emergency Fund

An emergency fund is one of the most important financial safety nets you can have. It's money set aside for unexpected events, like medical bills, car repairs, or job loss. Life is unpredictable, and having an emergency fund ensures that you won't have to rely on credit cards or loans in times of need. It's your cushion to keep you from falling into debt when things don't go as planned.

As soon as you've saved up 3-6 months' worth of living expenses, it's important to allocate that amount into an emergency fund. This fund acts as your safety net, giving you peace of mind in case of unexpected events like a job loss or a medical emergency.

Once your emergency fund is set up, you have a few options for where to keep it. You could leave it in a regular account without investing it, but over time, inflation will cause its value to depreciate, meaning your money will lose buying power. A smarter choice is to place your emergency fund in low-risk, low-return options, like a high-yield savings account, a money market account, or other secure financial instruments.

The key is to prioritize safety and accessibility—these funds should be easy to access when you need them but still earn a small return through interest or other low-risk growth. This way, your emergency fund not only maintains its value but also grows a little over time, helping offset the effects of inflation.

By choosing the right place to store your emergency fund, you're ensuring it remains a reliable safety net while also making your money work for you. This approach builds a strong foundation for both short-term security and long-term financial stability.

Take a moment to think about your comfort level when it comes to managing risk. Are you someone who's open to a little low-risk growth to combat inflation, or do you feel most secure playing it as safe as possible? Either choice is okay, as long as you understand one crucial fact: over time, the value of money decreases due to inflation.

For example, the $1,000 you have today won't hold the same value in 20 years. With inflation averaging around 3% per year, that $1,000 would only have the buying power of about $550 two decades from now—nearly half its current value gone. However, if that same $1,000 were in an investment earning a modest 3.5% annual return, it could grow to about $1,800 in 20 years. This small, steady growth helps your money outpace inflation and retain its value.

That's why placing your emergency fund in something like a high-yield savings account, a bond, or another low-risk investment can make such a big difference. It's not just about keeping your money safe—it's about ensuring it works quietly in the background, preserving its power for when you need it most.

Saving is Your Super Power

When it comes to achieving financial freedom, saving is one of the most important but often overlooked steps. Many people think of saving as just cutting back on their spending, but it's much more than that. Saving is about creating opportunities, building stability, and giving yourself the freedom to make choices in all areas of your life.

Saving is the cornerstone of financial independence. It helps create a financial cushion that protects you in case of emergencies, such as medical issues, job loss, or sudden expenses. Without this safety net, even small setbacks can cause big problems. Savings also provide the initial capital to start investing in things like stocks, real estate, or even a side business. With savings in place, you can also take smart risks, like switching careers or starting your own business, knowing that you have a financial backup plan.

The skill of saving is more than just putting money aside; it can help you in many areas of your life. Learning to save teaches you how to plan ahead and stay patient—qualities that are useful far beyond managing your money.

When you save, you learn how to think about the future and stay committed to your goals, even when the results aren't immediate. This same skill can help you achieve success in other parts of your life, whether it's working on a personal project, learning something new, or improving your health. Saving teaches you to focus on long-term goals, rather than getting distracted by short-term desires.

Saving also helps you practice patience and the ability to wait for a bigger reward. In other areas of life, like your career or relationships, the same idea applies. Sometimes, building a successful career means putting in hard work for a while before seeing the rewards, or nurturing relationships takes time and effort, but the results are worth it.

Additionally, when you have savings, you feel more confident about making decisions. With some financial security, you're not as afraid to take risks or try new things. Whether it's changing careers, moving to a new place, or pursuing something you've always wanted to do, having money saved up gives you the freedom to make these choices with less stress.

In short, saving is about more than just money. It helps you develop the ability to plan, stay focused, be patient, and make better decisions. These skills are useful not only in managing your money but in all areas of your life.

In your job, you'll likely find areas where money is being spent inefficiently—these are financial leaks. For example, you might notice unnecessary expenses like overordering supplies, inefficient use of resources, or missed opportunities to cut costs. As you develop your saving and money management skills, you'll start recognizing these leaks more easily.

Once you spot them, take action. Look for ways to reduce waste, streamline processes, or negotiate better deals. For instance, if you're in charge of office supplies, you could track usage and find bulk purchasing options to lower costs. Or, if there's a project running over budget, you could suggest more efficient ways to allocate funds.

By actively identifying and fixing these leaks, you're not only saving the company money but also proving your ability to think strategically about finances. This will show your value to the team and could lead to more responsibility or even promotions.

Being proactive in identifying and solving financial issues at work will also sharpen your money management skills. The more you practice recognizing and addressing financial inefficiencies, the better you'll become at managing your own money in everyday life. This is a practical skill that will help you improve your financial situation both at work and at home.

Investing in Yourself First

Saving is an important first step, but saving alone won't lead to financial freedom—this is where investing and putting your money to work come into play. Investing allows your money to grow over time, turning it into a powerful tool for building lasting wealth. It's not just about keeping money in the bank; it's about making those funds work for you through options like stocks, bonds, real estate, or even starting your own business.

The key is understanding your risk appetite and how much effort you're willing to put in. Some investments, like stocks and bonds, might require less hands-on work but carry varying levels of risk. Others, like real estate or starting a business, may demand more time and effort but could offer higher rewards.

Balancing these factors and choosing what aligns with your financial goals and comfort level is crucial. By putting your money to work in ways that suit you, you're taking the next step toward building a more secure and prosperous future.

Investing in oneself is one of the most impactful ways to lay the foundation for financial freedom. It's a thoughtful approach that often yields faster and more significant returns compared to other investments. This could involve enrolling in well-recognized courses to develop new skills, advancing in a career, or improving areas that enhance income potential or overall quality of life. High-quality courses have the power to save years of trial and error by providing clear, actionable strategies, while transformative books can offer timeless wisdom and proven methods for success.

For example, the *Rule #1 Investing* group by Phil Town has been a transformative resource for me and for many individuals seeking to understand the principles of value investing. Inspired by the legendary Warren Buffett, this approach focuses on identifying and investing in businesses that offer long-term value. Phil Town's method breaks down complex financial concepts into digestible strategies, making it an excellent starting point for beginners who want to build confidence and clarity in their investing journey.

Additionally, *The Intelligent Investor* by Benjamin Graham, often referred to as the "bible of investing," provides timeless lessons on financial markets, emphasizing the importance of discipline, patience, and a long-term perspective. Its principles have stood the test of time, guiding investors through market fluctuations and economic changes. These insights are particularly valuable for those aiming to develop a resilient, well-informed approach to managing their investments.

While there are countless resources available, this course and book are just two examples of tools that can help you enter the world of investing with a solid foundation. This isn't a paid endorsement, but rather a recognition of how helpful and practical Phil Town's *Rule #1 Investing* course can be, especially for beginners. It simplifies the learning process, offering a step-by-step guide to understanding the stock market, identifying profitable investments, and applying these lessons effectively.

Investing in the right educational resources, whether it's courses, books, or other learning tools, can make a significant difference in your financial journey. They equip you with the knowledge and confidence to take actionable steps toward building wealth. Remember, the key is to find resources that resonate with your goals and risk tolerance and to continuously expand your understanding as you progress. Strategically investing in personal growth ensures a lifetime of compounding benefits, equipping you with the knowledge and skills to achieve both financial and personal success.

Compound Effect

If you choose to read only one chapter of this book, let it be this one — because mastering the compound effect could be the single most life-changing shift you ever make. Imagine planting a single seed and watching it grow into a massive tree that produces fruit season after season. That's the magic of the compound effect — small, consistent actions that grow into significant results over time. While it may seem slow at first, the growth accelerates as time passes, and before you know it, you're reaping the rewards far beyond your initial efforts.

Money: Turning $500 a Month Into a Million-Dollar Fortune. If you had invested $500 every month for the past 30 years in the S&P 500, with an average annual return of about 10%, you'd have over **$1 million** today. It's not magic — it's math. The early years might feel slow, but as compound growth kicks in, your money starts to grow on top of itself. Each dollar earns returns, and those returns earn more returns. By the final years, the growth is exponential, far outpacing your contributions. This is the power of patience and persistence.

Knowledge: Reading Just 30 Minutes a Day Can Change Your Life. Imagine reading for just 30 minutes every day. On average, people can read about 20-30 pages in that time, depending on the book. Over a year, that's more than 180 hours of reading. If the average non-fiction book has 250 pages, you'd complete around 24 books per year. Now, imagine if most of those books were on personal finance, investing, and self-growth. The knowledge you'd accumulate would be life-changing. Knowledge compounds in your mind forever. The ideas, skills, and mental frameworks you acquire today can help you make better decisions tomorrow, next year, and for decades to come.

Other Areas Where Small Daily Actions Compound. The compound effect isn't limited to money and knowledge. It's a universal principle that can be applied to almost every part of your life. Here are a few other areas where small daily actions can lead to massive, long-term results:

1. **Health and Fitness**: Spend just 20-30 minutes a day exercising, and over the course of a year, you'll have worked out for over 180 hours. That's the equivalent of a full week's worth of focused health investment. Imagine the transformation your body and mind would experience with that kind of consistent effort.
2. **Skill Building:** Want to learn a new language, develop coding skills, or master public speaking? Commit to 20 minutes of practice each day. In a year, you'll have invested over 120 hours into that skill. Small, consistent effort can make you proficient in something that once seemed impossible.
3. **Relationships:** Consistently spending quality time with loved ones — even if it's just 10 minutes of undivided attention daily — can strengthen relationships that might otherwise weaken. A small daily investment of time in your relationships builds trust, love, and deep connection.
4. **Personal Growth**: Take 10 minutes each day to reflect, journal, or meditate. While 10 minutes might not seem life-changing, it's 60 hours a year spent gaining clarity, reducing stress, and improving your mindset. It's an investment in your mental well-being, and the returns are immeasurable.

The beauty of the compound effect is that you don't have to do anything monumental to see life-changing results. The small, daily choices you make — the $500 invested, the 30 minutes of reading, the 20 minutes of exercise — have the power to shape your future in ways you can't yet see. It's not about perfection or making a giant leap all at once. It's about staying consistent, even when it feels like nothing is happening. Because with compounding, it's not the first few steps that matter most — it's the momentum that builds over time.

Start small. Stay consistent. Watch the magic unfold.

ETFs vs Individual Stocks

When it comes to investing, there are many paths you can take, and two of the most popular options are ETFs (Exchange-Traded Funds) and individual stocks. The choice between the two depends largely on your risk tolerance and long-term financial goals. Before diving into this topic, let me clarify: I'm not a financial advisor. I'm simply sharing my personal experience to help you understand the key differences between investing in individual stocks and ETFs (Exchange-Traded Funds). Always do your own research or consult a professional before making investment decisions.

Individual Stocks can be more lucrative, especially when you're able to spot a strong company early on. Take the case of Ronald James Read, a simple janitor and gas station attendant who amassed a fortune of over $8 million through smart, long-term investments. He wasn't a Wall Street professional or a high-income earner. Instead, he followed the simple principle of investing in well-established, reliable companies such as Procter & Gamble and Johnson & Johnson. Read didn't try to chase the next big stock or time the market—he just bought stocks in solid companies and held them for decades. His story is a testament to the power of patience and the value of understanding that investing isn't about quick wins, but steady, long-term growth.

While this story may sound inspiring, it's important to remember that individual stocks carry more risk than ETFs. A single stock's value can fluctuate dramatically, and it's challenging to predict which companies will outperform. It's also time-consuming to research and track individual stocks, which is why they may not be the best option for beginners or those who don't have the time to actively monitor their investments.

On the other hand, ETFs provide a more diversified approach. When you invest in an ETF, you're buying a basket of stocks that may include companies from multiple industries, regions, and sectors. A perfect example is the S&P 500 ETF, which represents 500 of the largest companies in the U.S. By investing in an ETF, you're spreading out your risk and reducing the chances of a single poor-performing stock dragging down your entire portfolio. Over time, ETFs typically show steady growth, making them a solid choice for those who are in it for the long haul.

When it comes to investing in individual stocks, timing plays a significant role. The price of a stock can fluctuate, and depending on when you buy, you could be investing at a peak, when the price is high, or at a valley, when it's low. This is why timing can be a challenge. If you buy at a high and an economic downturn happens shortly after, your investment might lose value for years before it recovers. For example, if you invested just before the 2008 financial crisis, your stocks could have taken a major hit. If you were only thinking about the short term, you could have been left in a tough spot.

However, this is where long-term thinking comes into play. If you hold onto your investment long enough, you give it time to recover and grow as the economy stabilizes. Stocks often experience cycles of ups and downs, but over time, they tend to appreciate. This is why patience is key when investing in individual stocks. You must give your investments enough time to recover from downturns and reach their full potential.

One important thing to remember is that if you have your emergency fund in place, you can avoid being forced to sell your stocks during a downturn. This is why having a solid emergency fund is crucial—if unexpected expenses arise, you won't be forced to sell your investments at the worst possible time. When you have financial security in place, you can afford to keep your investments for the long haul, allowing them to grow without worrying about immediate cash needs.

This is why, in my opinion, ETFs are often a safer, more secure investment option. While individual stocks can offer high returns, they also carry more risk, particularly when trying to time the market. ETFs, on the other hand, provide diversification, which can reduce the impact of a single company's poor performance. By investing in ETFs over the long term, you give your money time to grow and recover from inevitable downturns. By keeping your emergency fund separate, you can invest 100% of your money in these long-term opportunities without the fear of needing to access it early. With proper planning, you can build wealth steadily and securely, without being forced to make panic-driven decisions.

This is a topic we could explore for hours because there's so much nuance, from the variety of ETFs available to the strategies for selecting individual stocks. But if we distill it down, the key takeaway is this: individual stocks demand time, analysis, and a tolerance for higher risk, while ETFs offer simplicity, diversification, and steady long-term returns with less effort. The right choice depends on your goals, time, and risk tolerance—so weigh the pros and cons carefully and choose the option that aligns best with your needs and lifestyle.

Launch Your Path

One of the most exciting paths to financial independence is starting your own business. It doesn't always require a huge upfront investment. With the right strategy, passion, and effort, you can turn a simple idea into a thriving business.

Here's the truth: success in business isn't just about having a great idea—it's about taking action, learning from the best, and building smart systems to keep everything running smoothly. I've personally experienced this in my real estate journey. I invested over $1,000 in real estate training, and it was a total game-changer. This investment allowed me to cut through the noise, avoid rookie mistakes, and fast-track my success. I started generating income so much faster than I would have on my own. This approach isn't unique to real estate—it works in any industry.

Here's a practical way to get started: If you're thinking about launching a business in a specific niche—like e-commerce, real estate, or consulting—don't leave it up to guesswork. Instead, approach it like a detective. Head to Google and search for training providers or courses in that space. But don't jump on the first shiny ad you see. Take your time to do some digging.

Here are some practical steps to make sure the training is legit and worth your money:

1. Investigate Reviews and Ratings. Start with trusted review platforms like Trustpilot, Google Reviews, and Reddit communities related to your niche. Look at both the glowing 5-star reviews *and* the critical 1-star reviews. Sometimes, those 1-star reviews can reveal red flags about poor support, hidden fees, or overpromised results. But don't write off a course just because it has a few negative reviews—people love to complain. Look for patterns. If multiple people mention the same issue (like "support is terrible" or "content is outdated"), that's a sign to pause and reconsider.

2. Look for Real Success Stories (Not Just Testimonials). Many courses will parade "success stories" on their websites. But don't be fooled by polished marketing. Real success stories will often show *specific, measurable outcomes*—like "I made my first $1,000 in 30 days" or "I closed my first real estate deal within 3 months." Go beyond the testimonials provided by the course itself. Look for people who mention the course in Facebook groups, Reddit threads, or YouTube reviews. If you can, reach out to them and ask, "Hey, was it really worth it?" This small step can prevent you from wasting hundreds (or thousands) of dollars.

3. Check the Instructor's Track Record. Don't just trust the "guru" because they look good on camera. Research their background. Do they have real-world experience in the field they're teaching, or are they just "selling how to sell courses"? Look at their LinkedIn profile, see if they've built successful businesses themselves, and find out if they've been featured on reputable platforms, podcasts, or interviews. If the instructor has only ever made money selling courses, that's a red flag.

4. Ask About Ongoing Support and Community. Great training doesn't stop with the last lesson. Check if the course offers live Q&A sessions, discussion forums, or access to a student community. Having a network of people on the same journey as you can provide extra guidance and motivation. Ask questions like:

- Is there lifetime access to course materials?
- Are there live support calls or direct access to the instructor?
- Is there a student group (like a Facebook or Discord community) where I can connect with others?

Support can be a huge part of your success. If something isn't clear in the course, you'll want a way to ask questions.

5. Look for "Try Before You Buy" Options. Does the course offer a free trial, preview, or refund policy? If not, that's a yellow flag. Most reputable courses offer at least a sneak peek of what's inside. Check if you can see the curriculum layout, lesson previews, or sample content. If they have a refund policy, read the fine print. Some will claim "money-back guarantee," but only if you complete 90% of the course and submit assignments. Know the details upfront.

6. Check for Certifications or Recognized Partnerships. Some courses have partnerships with industry-recognized organizations. If you see logos from reputable brands, universities, or government initiatives, that's a good sign. Certifications can also add value to your resume or business, especially in fields like project management, finance, or tech.

7. Follow the Instructor or Course Provider Online. Before you buy, follow the instructor on social media. Look at their free content. If they're constantly giving high-value insights, their paid course is probably even better. But if all you see is flashy sales pitches, that might be a sign they care more about selling courses than providing real value.

8. Ask Yourself: Do They Practice What They Preach?. Does the person running a "How to Start a Real Estate Empire" course actually *own real estate*? If not, that's a problem. If someone is teaching "How to Start an Online Business," but they've never run a business themselves (besides selling courses), that's another red flag. Look for transparency. True experts share their wins, losses, and lessons learned along the way.

9. Verify the Course's "Guarantees". Many training providers make big promises like "Get rich in 90 days" or "Guaranteed to double your income." Be skeptical of these guarantees. Check for loopholes in the refund policy and see if it's even realistic.

If the offer sounds too good to be true, it probably is. Look for courses that promote *skills* over *results*—because no course can "guarantee" your success.

10. Take a Test Drive with Free Content. A good course creator won't hide all their knowledge behind a paywall. See if they offer free mini-courses, webinars, or YouTube videos where they share useful insights. If the free content is valuable, chances are the paid course will be even better. If their free content is vague, the paid course might just be more of the same.

If you're serious about achieving financial freedom, starting a business can be a great path to get there. But instead of copying someone else's plan, focus on building a business that fits *your* goals and what matters most to *you*.

Think about what excites you. Are you interested in real estate? Do you love the idea of creating and selling products? Or do you have a skill you could turn into a service? The best business idea for you is the one that sparks your passion and aligns with your long-term dreams. If you're not sure where to start, here are some proven ideas that have worked for me and countless others.

Airbnb and Short-Term Rentals

Starting an Airbnb or short-term rental business doesn't have to be a massive investment. In fact, it's one of the most accessible ways to step into the world of real estate. You don't need to buy a whole property to get started — many people begin by renting out a spare room or subleasing an apartment (just be sure to check your lease and local laws first). It's a smart way to dip your toes into the rental market without taking on huge risks.

Before jumping in, it's a good idea to do some research on your local market. Look around your city or town — are there areas that attract tourists, business travelers, or visiting families? Places near popular attractions, hospitals, or universities tend to have strong demand for short-term rentals. A quick search on Airbnb can give you insight into how much similar properties are charging and how often they're booked. Knowing the market puts you in a stronger position to set the right price and maximize your bookings.

Here's an important step that often gets overlooked: check local regulations. Some cities require hosts to get permits or licenses, while others limit the number of days you can rent out your property. It's worth taking a moment to look this up so you don't run into issues down the line. And if you're subleasing, be sure to check with your landlord to avoid any surprises. These simple steps can save you a lot of headaches later.

Once you have a property ready to go, it's time to make it shine. People love staying in places that feel warm, clean, and thoughtfully put together. A few small touches — like fresh linens, fast Wi-Fi, a coffee station, and cozy decor — can turn a simple space into one that people love (and leave 5-star reviews for). You don't have to go overboard, but creating a clean, welcoming space can make all the difference.

Now, let's talk about photos — they are EVERYTHING. Guests will scroll through dozens of listings, and your photos are your first impression. Bright, clear, high-quality images can make your place stand out. Use natural lighting if you can, and if your budget allows, consider hiring a photographer (Airbnb even offers this service in some locations). It's a small investment that can pay off big time by bringing in more bookings.

Your listing description is your chance to show off the personality of your space. Be honest but also make it sound appealing. Instead of saying, "Small apartment," try, "Cozy Urban Escape Close to Downtown Adventures." Highlight key features like free parking, a dedicated workspace, or proximity to tourist spots. Your goal is to make people imagine themselves staying there.

To save yourself time and make things feel more "hands-off," automation is your best friend. Tools like Smartbnb (now called Hospitable) allow you to send automated messages to guests. That means you won't have to answer every single question about check-in or house rules — it's all done for you. This makes life easier for you and creates a better guest experience. Win-win!

Speaking of guest experience, this part matters *a lot*. Your goal is to get glowing 5-star reviews because they boost your listing in Airbnb's search results (which means more bookings for you). Be responsive, keep the space spotless, and handle any issues with kindness and urgency. Happy guests leave happy reviews, and those reviews help you attract even more bookings.

The best part? Once you have everything set up, your rental can become a source of passive income. Imagine having systems in place so that even when you're on vacation, your rental is still generating cash. You can hire a cleaning service to handle turnovers, use pricing tools like Pricelabs to automatically adjust your rates, and automate guest communication. The goal is to have your rental business run smoothly with as little of your time as possible.

If you enjoy the process, you can expand! Start with one property, master the process, and then use your profits to get another. Before you know it, you could have a whole portfolio of short-term rentals generating passive income. It's a strategy that's worked for many people — and it can work for you too if you approach it with patience, research, and a bit of strategy.

If this sounds like a path you'd love to explore, take the first step. Research your local market, check the rules, and see where you might be able to get started. It's a business model that's not only accessible but also incredibly rewarding once it's up and running. With the right systems and a little persistence, you'll be well on your way to building a reliable stream of income that works for you.

Online Businesses: Turning Passion into Profit

Starting an online business has never been more accessible. Thanks to platforms like Etsy, Shopify, and Amazon, you can sell products with minimal upfront costs. You don't need to own a warehouse or buy a ton of inventory. In fact, many people start with products they already have at home or by creating digital products like e-books, printables, or online courses. The beauty of an online business is its flexibility — you can run it from anywhere, and it works around your schedule.

The first step is figuring out *what* you want to sell. This is where passion and strategy meet. Think about your strengths, interests, or skills. Do you love crafting or DIY projects? Etsy could be your perfect fit. Have a knack for digital design? Sell e-books or templates on Gumroad. Know a product that people are constantly searching for? Source it through drop shipping and sell it on Shopify. If you're not sure what to sell, do a little research on what's trending in your niche. Tools like Google Trends or Etsy's search bar can give you an idea of what people are actively looking for.

Once you've chosen your product, it's time to set up your online store. Fortunately, platforms like Shopify make this super easy with step-by-step guides. You don't need to be a tech wizard or a coding expert. Just pick a template, customize it to match your brand, and upload product photos. Speaking of photos — just like with Airbnb, good visuals make all the difference. Take bright, clear pictures that show off every detail of your product. Customers can't hold your product in their hands, so your images have to *do the talking*.

Your store is live — now what? It's time to market it. This is where many people get stuck, but it doesn't have to be overwhelming. Start with social media. Platforms like Instagram, TikTok, and Pinterest are goldmines for product-based businesses. Share behind-the-scenes moments, customer reviews, or videos of your product in action. Short, engaging videos (like TikToks or Reels) have the power to bring thousands of new eyeballs to your store.

If you have a little extra cash, you can experiment with paid ads. Facebook and Google Ads allow you to target your ideal customers with pinpoint accuracy. But if you're on a budget, focus on organic marketing first. Building an email list is also a smart move. Offer a freebie (like a discount or a helpful guide) in exchange for people's email addresses. Email marketing has one of the *highest returns on investment (ROI)* of any marketing strategy.

Over time, as your online business grows, you can start automating parts of it. Use apps that send abandoned cart reminders to customers who almost bought but didn't. Set up auto-replies to customer questions. Even product shipping can be outsourced through fulfillment services, so you're not stuck packaging boxes all day. The ultimate goal is to create a business that runs smoothly without needing your constant attention.

Don't underestimate the potential here. People have gone from selling handmade candles in their living rooms to running full-fledged online empires. The opportunity is real. If you're willing to put in the effort to find the right product, build a small but loyal customer base, and create simple systems, you could be earning money online while you sleep. The key is to start small, learn from every step, and *keep going*.

Freelance Consulting: Turn Your Skills Into a Business

If you have a skill, there's a good chance someone out there is willing to pay for it. That's the magic of freelancing and consulting. Unlike traditional jobs, you get to set your own rates, choose your clients, and work on projects that interest you. With just a laptop and an internet connection, you can build a business offering your skills to the world.

So, where do you start? The first step is identifying your *superpower*. What do people come to you for advice about? Are you great at graphic design, writing, coding, marketing, or social media? Maybe you have a knack for organizing or coaching others. That one skill you take for granted might be exactly what someone else is looking for. If you're unsure, ask friends or colleagues, "What do you think I'm really good at?" Their answers might surprise you.

Once you've pinpointed your skill, it's time to package it into a service. This part is easier than it sounds. Let's say you're a graphic designer. You could offer logo design, brand kits, or social media templates. If you're a writer, you could specialize in blog posts, website copy, or email marketing. Take your big, broad skill (like "design") and break it down into specific services (like "social media graphics"). This makes it easier for clients to see exactly what they're paying for.

Next, you'll want to get your first client. The easiest way to do this is by tapping into your existing network. Let your friends, family, and former colleagues know that you're offering your services. You can also use platforms like Upwork, Fiverr, or LinkedIn to connect with people looking for help. These platforms are competitive, but if you position yourself well and deliver great work, you'll stand out. When you're just starting, it's okay to offer a small discount or a "starter package" to get that first testimonial. Once you have reviews, you can raise your rates with confidence.

Pricing your services can be tricky, but here's a simple tip: Start by calculating how much you want to earn in a month. Divide that number by how many hours you're willing to work. This gives you a base hourly rate. But don't stop there. As you get more experience and stronger testimonials, raise your rates. High-quality clients don't just look for "cheap" — they look for *expertise* and *reliability*.

Now, let's talk systems. When you have multiple clients and deadlines, things can get messy *fast*. That's why having a system to track projects, deadlines, and invoices is essential. Tools like Trello, ClickUp, or Asana can keep you organized. Platforms like PayPal, Stripe, or HoneyBook make invoicing and payment collection easy. With good systems in place, you can avoid the overwhelm that often comes with freelancing.

Want to make freelancing even better? Aim to create *retainer clients*. Instead of getting paid for one-off projects, work with clients who pay you monthly to handle ongoing tasks. This could mean managing their social media, updating their website, or writing regular blog posts. Retainers give you steady, predictable income every month — something every freelancer dreams of.

Once you've built a steady client base, you can think about *scaling* your freelance business. Scaling doesn't always mean hiring employees. It could mean offering higher-priced premium services, creating online courses, or offering group coaching. For example, if you're a marketing consultant, you could create a course on "How to Launch Your First Facebook Ad Campaign." This way, you're no longer trading hours for dollars.

Freelancing isn't just about making money — it's about *freedom*. You can choose to work 20 hours a week or 50. You can work from home, a cafe, or a beach. You have control over your schedule and your growth. It takes effort to build it, but once it's running smoothly, you'll realize just how powerful it is to have skills that pay the bills.

The ultimate goal of any side hustle—whether it's Airbnb, freelancing, or an online business—is to eventually turn it into a self-sustaining system that works for you, not the other way around. Instead of doing every task yourself, focus on building processes that can be automated or delegated. For an Airbnb business, you can automate guest check-ins with smart locks, use cleaning services, and set up automated guest communication. In freelancing, you can hire subcontractors to handle smaller tasks or use project management tools to streamline workflows. For online businesses, tools like e-commerce automation, customer support chatbots, and order fulfillment services can free up your time. The shift from being "the worker" to "the CEO" happens when you build systems, hire help, and oversee operations from a higher level—only stepping in to monitor and make adjustments. This approach allows you to grow your income streams while reclaiming your time.

The journey to financial freedom is different for everyone, so it's important to pick a path that fits your skills, interests, and lifestyle goals. This could be Airbnb rentals, online businesses, or anything else. Take the first step today — your future self will thank you!

5

Investing Beyond Money

True financial freedom is not just about building wealth — it's about building a fulfilling life. Throughout this book, we've emphasized that the journey to financial independence should not come at the cost of happiness. Happiness is not something you find at the finish line; it's something you cultivate along the way. Reaching financial freedom should be seen as a way to amplify the joy, peace, and purpose you've already created in your life. Once you've achieved your financial goals, it's essential to sustain them by maintaining the habits and mindset that got you there. True success is not just about having more money — it's about having more meaning, and that's a form of wealth that no market fluctuation can ever take away

Start With Happiness Now

Earlier in this book, I mentioned something important: that in order to truly pursue financial freedom, you need to start with being happy right now—before you even think about the money. This might sound counterintuitive at first, but it's a psychological hack that has worked wonders for many people, myself included. It's something I learned from my therapist, and it's truly a game-changer when it comes to not only achieving financial freedom but living a more fulfilled life overall.

Why does this "happy already" mindset serve you better than a "lack" mindset? Well, it's simple: when you come from a place of abundance and contentment, you attract more opportunities, ideas, and energy to create the life you want. On the other hand, when you're constantly focused on what you don't have or what's missing, it's easy to feel stuck, stressed, or overwhelmed, which can block the path to achieving your goals.

A "lack" mindset makes you feel like there's never enough—whether it's money, time, or opportunities—and it keeps you in a constant state of anxiety. You might feel like you need to hustle harder or sacrifice more, but this often leads to burnout and frustration. When you shift to a "happy already" mindset, you're telling yourself that you have everything you need to be successful. It helps you approach challenges with calm and confidence rather than desperation. Instead of worrying about what you don't have, you focus on what's going well and what you can control right now.

This shift in mindset isn't just wishful thinking. It's a practical and powerful way to rewire your brain for success. By starting each day from a place of gratitude and joy, you're more likely to make decisions that align with your long-term goals. You'll feel more motivated, more productive, and more open to the opportunities that come your way. And when it comes to finances, the "happy already" mindset is incredibly powerful. It helps you stay grounded and avoid making impulsive financial decisions based on fear or scarcity.

To enhance this mindset every day, here's a simple routine that can make a huge difference:

Morning Gratitude. Start each day by listing at least three things you're grateful for (add more with time). They can be small or big—anything that brings you joy or peace. Gratitude shifts your focus from what you lack to what you have, helping you start the day on a positive note. This sets the tone for the rest of your day.

Loud message to your brain. It's a scientific fact that your brain responds much better when you speak your goals out loud rather than just thinking them in your head. That's the secret behind the power of positive affirmations. When you vocalize your goals and aspirations, you're not only reinforcing them in your mind, but you're also engaging the emotional and sensory parts of your brain that are crucial for making them a reality.

Speaking your affirmations aloud creates a deeper connection to your desired outcome. It helps you feel the energy of your goals and builds confidence in achieving them. You're programming your brain to believe in your success, making it easier to take the actions needed to get there.

So, take a moment each day to say your affirmations out loud. Speak with conviction, as though these goals are already yours. Whether you're saying, "I am financially free," "I attract wealth and abundance," or "I am in control of my financial future," saying these words with intention will powerfully align your mind and actions. It's like planting seeds in your mind that will grow into the results you desire!

If you think you don't have time for this, here's a good example: think about those moments when you're stuck in a car jam or waiting in line. Instead of letting those minutes go to waste or filling them with frustration, you can use that time to repeat your affirmations. It's a simple and effective way to make use of any downtime during the day, turning it into a productive and empowering moment.

Mindfulness. One of the most powerful ways to start your day on the right foot is by practicing mindfulness or meditation. This helps clear your mind, reduce stress, and set a calm tone for the rest of the day. My favorite app for this is Calm, but there are plenty of other great options available as well, such as Headspace and Insight Timer. Each app offers guided meditations and mindfulness practices that are perfect for both beginners and experienced practitioners.

By setting aside just 10-15 minutes each morning, you'll be able to create a peaceful mental space, reduce any anxiety about the day ahead, and help sharpen your focus. Whether it's through calming music, breathing exercises, or guided visualizations, starting your day with mindfulness will have a profound impact on your overall mindset and energy. The beauty of these apps is their simplicity and accessibility, allowing you to take a moment for yourself, no matter how busy your schedule may be.

Visualization is a powerful tool for bridging the gap between where you are now and where you want to be. If you have just a few more minutes a day, give this practice a try—you'll be amazed at the difference it makes. As a next-level power, it acts as a super-enhancer of mindfulness, gratitude, and positive affirmations, significantly boosting your success rate. By vividly imagining your ideal future, you align your thoughts, emotions, and actions with your deepest goals, creating a mental blueprint for success. Adding daily reflection to your evening routine helps you gain clarity and create a habit of continuous improvement. Benjamin Franklin famously embraced this practice by developing a structured routine that included reflecting on his day every evening. This is how it looks.

Visualization. After your morning meditation, take a few minutes to close your eyes and vividly imagine the life you want to create. The more colorful and detailed your visualization, the more powerful it becomes. Picture yourself already living your dreams—whether that's achieving financial freedom, growing your business, or spending more time with your family. Engage all of your senses in this exercise: feel the emotions of success, hear the sounds of your accomplishments, and even imagine the scents and textures around you. How does it feel to be in that moment? What does your environment look like? What are the people around you saying? The more real and sensory-rich your visualization, the stronger the connection you create to your goals. Doing this right after meditation helps you to maintain a calm, focused mind while aligning your intentions for the day with your long-term vision. This practice reinforces the belief that you can and will achieve what you desire.

End of Day Reflection. The end of your day is a mighty time for reflection. It's when you can process what went well and what didn't, and where you can grow. By taking a few minutes to reflect each evening, you gain clarity about your actions and set yourself up for success the next day. Here are some practical examples to help you get started with your end-of-day reflection:

- **What Went Well Today?** Begin by celebrating your wins, no matter how small. It could be as simple as sticking to your budget for the day, investing in yourself with a short course, or even managing your emotions in a stressful situation. Recognizing these wins boosts your confidence and reinforces your ability to succeed. For instance, if you've been focusing on saving, even setting aside a small amount can be a win. Acknowledge how these steps, no matter how small, are getting you closer to your financial goals.

- **What Could Have Gone Better?** Next, think about areas where you could improve. Maybe you didn't stick to your planned budget, or perhaps you missed a chance to practice mindfulness. This isn't about beating yourself up; it's about seeing where you can grow. Be gentle with yourself and ask, "What can I do differently tomorrow to make progress?" For example, if you overspent, you might reflect on why that happened—was it impulse shopping? Did you forget about a need in your budget? This gives you actionable insights on how to adjust.

- **What Did I Learn Today?** Reflecting on the lessons learned is key to progress. You might have gained new knowledge from reading, a course, or from a conversation you had. For instance, you might have read about different investment strategies and realized you want to start looking into ETFs more seriously. Or perhaps a conversation made you think about your goals from a new perspective. Write these down so you can remember them. This reflection not only helps you retain what you learned but also builds momentum for your future growth.

- **Gratitude Practice**. End your reflection by noting three things you're grateful for. Gratitude shifts your mindset from scarcity to abundance, helping you stay motivated and positive. Perhaps you're grateful for your ability to save even when it's difficult, the support of a friend or mentor, or the progress you've made toward your career goals. A daily gratitude practice is a reminder that even when challenges arise, there's always something to be thankful for.

- **Plan for Tomorrow.** Finish your reflection by setting one or two actionable goals for the next day. It could be as simple as reviewing your budget, scheduling time to work on your side hustle, or taking an hour to learn something new. Having clear, small goals for the next day keeps you moving forward and ensures that you're not starting your day feeling overwhelmed or directionless. Planning also makes your next morning more productive and less stressful.

By incorporating this routine into your daily life, you can cultivate a "happy already" mindset that supports your financial journey. Remember, true financial freedom isn't just about accumulating wealth—it's about finding joy and contentment throughout the process. When you approach your goals from a place of happiness and abundance, you'll be more likely to achieve them with greater ease and fulfillment.

In just 30 minutes a day, you're setting yourself up for long-term success—and the best part? This is all within your reach! With a small, consistent daily routine like this, you'll see incredible results over time. It may seem like a little effort each day, but over time, those small actions will add up to something truly remarkable. Consistency is key, and making this part of your daily life is one of the best ways to create lasting positive change.

Sustaining Financial Freedom

One of the simplest, most effective ways to stay on top of your finances is by creating a financial calendar. This is the backbone of your financial success—it's a tool to help you manage your income, investments, taxes, and other key financial events. It's something you can easily set up using tools you're already familiar with, like Google Calendar.

For example, you can schedule quarterly check-ins to review your investment portfolio. Set reminders for key financial dates—like when your taxes are due or when it's time to rebalance your portfolio. If you want to review your budget every month, mark it on your calendar. By creating these financial check-ins, you're turning your financial goals into concrete actions.

You can set recurring reminders for your monthly budget review, quarterly investment check-ins, or annual updates on your long-term financial goals. It keeps you organized and accountable without you having to worry about forgetting important dates. You'll get a notification, and boom—you're reminded to take action. This simple tool ensures you stay on track, stay informed, and make financial decisions with intention.

By blocking out time for these financial check-ins, you're consistently reviewing your progress, adjusting your strategy when necessary, and ensuring you're not falling behind.

If you want to stay on the path to lasting financial freedom, you need to regularly evaluate and update those goals. Life happens. Your circumstances will change, and so should your financial plan. Regularly revisiting your goals ensures that your plan stays in sync with your current situation and long-term vision.

Set a recurring reminder to review your goals every few months. Ask yourself: Are your investments on track? Do you need to adjust your savings goals due to unexpected changes in your income or expenses? What about your passive income? Is it growing as expected?

Your goals should evolve. If you've achieved a milestone, celebrate it—and then set a new, more ambitious goal. If something is taking longer than expected, adjust your timeline, but don't give up. Use your financial calendar to schedule these reviews so you're making this process an intentional part of your routine. The more often you assess and revise your goals, the more likely you are to stay on track and adapt to changing circumstances.

Evaluating your goals regularly is not just about tracking progress; it's about staying flexible and proactive. If you've experienced a windfall, consider reinvesting it to grow your wealth even faster. If you've had setbacks, don't despair—adjust your strategy and move forward. A fluid plan is a plan that works.

On your journey to financial freedom, there will be mistakes and setbacks. The key isn't avoiding them entirely—it's learning how to bounce back stronger and smarter. Some of the best lessons come from what doesn't work. Whether it's an investment that didn't pan out as expected, a business idea that didn't take off, or a financial strategy that fell short, these moments are growth opportunities.

The first thing to understand is that setbacks are not failures; they are stepping stones to success. Instead of getting discouraged or upset when things don't go as planned, focus on what you can learn from the situation. Maybe a particular investment didn't yield the expected return, or you underestimated a business risk. These are valuable learning experiences that can help you make more informed decisions going forward.

When something doesn't work out, take a moment to reflect on what went wrong. Ask yourself key questions like:

- **What could I have done differently?** Reflect on the steps that led to the outcome. Were there warning signs you missed? Did you make assumptions that weren't backed by enough research?
- **What can I learn from this experience?** Every setback carries a lesson. Maybe you learned that a certain investment strategy isn't a good fit for your risk tolerance, or perhaps a particular business approach requires more effort than you anticipated.
- **How can I apply this lesson going forward?** The most important step is using what you've learned to make smarter decisions in the future. Adjust your strategy, refine your approach, and move forward with the new knowledge you've gained.

For example, if an investment didn't work out, instead of focusing on the disappointment, analyze the factors that contributed to it. Was it the timing? The market conditions? Or perhaps the company's fundamentals weren't as solid as you thought? With this insight, you can adjust your investment criteria next time and make smarter, more calculated choices.

It's important to remember that investing and financial planning are not about avoiding mistakes—they're about minimizing them and learning from the ones that do happen. Keep in mind that all successful investors, entrepreneurs, and financial planners have faced setbacks along the way. The difference is that they didn't let those setbacks define them; they used them as stepping stones to refine their strategies and make smarter, more informed decisions.

The lesson here is clear: Don't be afraid of mistakes. Embrace them as opportunities to learn and grow. With each mistake, you'll become more knowledgeable, more skilled, and more prepared for the next opportunity that comes your way. As you continue your financial journey, the lessons learned from your missteps will become one of your most valuable assets, allowing you to make more intelligent decisions and ultimately move closer to your financial goals.

Stay resilient, stay focused, and remember: that what doesn't work is just another lesson on the path to success.

6

The Power of Structure: Designing Your Day

Starting your day with purpose sets the tone for everything that follows. A strong morning routine primes your mind and body for success, boosting focus, energy, and motivation. Afternoon rituals help maintain momentum, ensuring you stay productive rather than burning out. Evening routines are just as essential, allowing you to reflect, recharge, and prepare for the next day with clarity and intention. By designing a daily structure that works for you, you create a system that supports consistent progress toward your goals.

Morning: Start Your Day Right

Gratitude and Reflection (10 minutes): Start your day by taking a moment to focus on gratitude. Grab a journal or simply sit quietly, and mentally list three (or more) things you're grateful for. As you do this, allow yourself to feel the emotions behind each thing you're grateful for—whether it's the love of family, the roof over your head, or the opportunity to learn and grow. Let yourself experience the warmth of those feelings, the sense of fulfillment, and the peace that comes with recognizing the good in your life. After this, reflect on your financial goals. Visualize why financial freedom matters to you—how it would feel to live life on your terms, free from financial worry, able to spend more time with the people you love and invest in the things that truly bring you joy. The more vividly you can see and feel these emotions, the stronger your connection to your goals will be. This practice doesn't just set a positive tone for your day—it helps align your mindset, creating a deep sense of motivation and focus that carries through everything you do. The emotions you feel now will stay with you throughout the day, guiding your actions and decisions with purpose.

Plan Your Day (10 minutes): Take 10 minutes each morning to clearly outline your priorities—both personal and financial. Write down the specific tasks that will bring you closer to your goals. For example, if you're working on a side project, break down the steps you'll take today. If you're researching investments, decide what key action you'll focus on. Make sure to also account for staying focused at your current job—perhaps set specific time blocks for deep work and avoid distractions. Here's a challenge: add a 30-minute slot for financial learning to your plan. This could be reading, listening to a podcast, or researching investments. I'll explain in the next chapter how to easily make this happen with simple, proven tools to boost your work effectiveness. By having this roadmap, you'll stay on track and make sure everything you do aligns with your bigger goals. This simple daily habit ensures you're consistently working towards what truly matters.

By investing just 20 minutes each morning, you're setting the foundation for long-term success. These small, consistent steps may not feel like much at first, but remember, each day builds on the one before. Think of it like planting a seed—at first, you might not see immediate results, but with time and care, it grows into something substantial. This daily 20-minute commitment compounds over time, creating exponential growth. It might feel slow at the beginning, but when you look back after a month, you'll start to see the power of these small actions. Trust the process and be patient. It's not about making giant leaps overnight—it's about staying consistent. As you continue, you'll witness how those 20 minutes every morning can lead to tangible progress, bringing you closer to your bigger financial goals. Stay focused and dedicated, and soon enough, you'll be amazed at how much you've achieved with just a little effort each day. So, do yourself a favor for the future—wake up a little earlier, go to bed a little earlier, but find those 20 minutes. This small trick will work wonders and set you on the path to the life you want.

Afternoon: Keep Momentum

The very first thing you should do when you arrive at the office is take 10 minutes to plan your day. This isn't just about writing a list; it's about designing a blueprint for success. Brian Tracy, a master in effectiveness, teaches that the time you spend planning creates exponential returns by saving you time and energy during execution. Think about it—just 10 focused minutes can unlock hours of productive time that would otherwise slip through the cracks.

For busy parents, this is a lifesaver. Your evenings are often consumed by family responsibilities—helping with homework, cooking dinner, or getting everyone ready for bed. By reclaiming this time during your 9-to-5, you free yourself from the guilt of "not having enough time." And if you're someone who has downtime at home, let's be real—this makes it even easier to get started. You have the opportunity, so why not use it?

Here's how you make those 10 minutes count: start by outlining your priorities. Identify what truly matters today, both for your work and your personal goals. Focus on the tasks that will have the biggest impact and align them with your long-term vision. Use the 80/20 rule to determine the 20% of actions that will deliver 80% of the results. Maybe it's completing a key work task, preparing for a big meeting, or tackling a project that's been on your mind. Schedule these tasks, protect that time fiercely, and don't let distractions steal it away.

Speaking of distractions, they're everywhere. Checking emails, attending meetings that don't require your input, or lingering in conversations can quickly eat up your day. Instead, start batching similar tasks together. Handle all your emails in one block. Schedule calls back-to-back. Dive into deep work without interruptions. This focused approach doesn't just save time—it improves the quality of your work. Multitasking and constant task-switching can reduce productivity by as much as 40%. By eliminating these inefficiencies, you'll find yourself gaining valuable time without sacrificing results.

And what do you do with this newfound time? You invest it in yourself. Use those extra 30 minutes during your workday to focus on financial growth. Read about investing, watch a short video on personal finance, or dive into research on ETFs or other wealth-building strategies. This isn't just time spent; it's time multiplied.

Let's break it down:

- **Morning Planning (10 minutes):** Start your day with a clear focus. Map out the most important tasks and allocate time for them. This sets the tone for a productive day.
- **Execution Mode:** Stick to your plan, eliminate unnecessary distractions, and group similar tasks to create flow.
- **Financial Learning (30 minutes):** Use the time you've saved wisely. This can be a podcast over lunch, a few pages of a book after completing a major task, or some quiet research time mid-afternoon.

This method allows you to prioritize both your daily responsibilities and your long-term growth. If you're a parent balancing a packed schedule, this simple habit can shift your day without adding stress. And if you have free time at home, well, you've got even fewer excuses!

These small, intentional changes aren't just about saving time—they're about transforming it into something meaningful. With consistency, you'll find that these simple steps build momentum, helping you create the life you've always envisioned. Start today, because every minute matters.

Evening: Reflect & Grow

Your evening is an opportunity to reflect, recharge, and refocus. Whether you're a busy parent juggling home responsibilities or someone with more flexibility to invest in personal growth, this time can help solidify the progress you've made during the day.

If you're a parent, the evening often comes with a full plate of chores, bedtime routines, or helping kids with homework. Instead of seeing this as a limitation, let it be a moment of pride. You've already invested in yourself earlier in the day, whether through morning planning or dedicating 30 minutes to financial learning. Acknowledge your effort and thank yourself for staying committed to your goals. Let this sense of accomplishment fuel your joy as you spend quality time with your loved ones. Play, connect, and relax—you've earned this moment. These consistent daily actions, no matter how small, will add up to meaningful progress over time.

If you have more flexibility in your evening schedule, this is your golden chance to build on the foundation you laid during the day. Consider picking up a book that deepens your financial knowledge. Here are some excellent choices to start with:

- **The Intelligent Investor by Benjamin Graham:** This classic book is a must-read for anyone interested in value investing. Benjamin Graham, the mentor of Warren Buffett, explains how to evaluate stocks, understand market fluctuations, and invest with a margin of safety to minimize risk and maximize returns.

- **Rich Dad Poor Dad by Robert T. Kiyosaki:** A highly influential personal finance book, it contrasts the financial philosophies of Kiyosaki's "rich dad" and "poor dad." It teaches the importance of assets, financial education, and shifting your mindset from earning money to making your money work for you.
- **The Millionaire Next Door by Thomas J. Stanley and William D. Danko:** Based on extensive research, this book reveals the habits and characteristics of millionaires who quietly build wealth over time. It emphasizes frugality, hard work, and living below your means as key traits for financial success.
- **Think and Grow Rich by Napoleon Hill:** A timeless classic, this book explores the mindset and principles that successful individuals use to build wealth and achieve their goals. It focuses on the power of belief, persistence, and definitive purpose in creating financial and personal success.
- **Common Stocks and Uncommon Profits by Philip Fisher:** This book dives deep into the art of growth investing. Philip Fisher outlines how to analyze companies, evaluate their long-term prospects, and identify stocks that will provide exceptional returns. His advice remains relevant for modern investors.

Take 20–30 minutes to read, even if it's just a chapter. Over time, this small daily habit will lead to profound insights. Beyond books, explore other ways to expand your financial understanding. Podcasts, such as *BiggerPockets Money* or *We Study Billionaires,* are a great way to learn while relaxing or tidying up. If you prefer a more structured approach, consider enrolling in an online course on investing or financial planning. Platforms like Udemy or LinkedIn Learning offer a wide range of topics that you can work through at your own pace.

You can also turn to YouTube for shorter, focused lessons. Channels like Graham Stephan's provide valuable insights into personal finance and investing. If you're up for something interactive, look for local seminars or webinars, which are often free or affordable and provide opportunities to engage with experts.

At the end of your evening, reflect on what you've learned. Journaling one insight or action step not only helps you retain information but also keeps you aligned with your long-term goals.

By dedicating your evening to intentional growth—whether it's celebrating your wins, deepening your knowledge, or spending quality time with family—you're making the most of every moment. These deliberate choices will compound into the life you're working to create.

Staying Consistent and Focused

Staying consistent each day is the key to making meaningful progress. Here's how I structure my day to stay productive, focused and energized. It's simple, practical, and effective, and I truly hope it can add some value to your daily life too.

THE POWER OF STRUCTURE: DESIGNING YOUR DAY

I start my day at 5:30 AM, giving myself a quiet moment before the rest of the world wakes up. The first 30 minutes are dedicated to meditation and gratitude. I sit quietly, calm my mind, and then spend a few moments thinking about what I'm thankful for. This helps me start the day with a positive, clear mindset and boosts my energy for what's to come.

Next, I do 30 minutes of high-intensity exercise, like Tabata. It's short but intense, and it helps wake me up, get my blood pumping, and energize me for the day ahead. After exercise, I have my first espresso of the day. I wait until after my workout to have my coffee because science shows that drinking it first thing in the morning can mess with your body's natural cortisol levels. When you wake up, your cortisol is already high, and adding caffeine right away can disrupt that balance and cause jitters later. By waiting until after exercise, my body wakes up more naturally, and the coffee boosts my mood and adds a little extra joy to my day—I just love the taste! It's my small reward after a productive start.

Then, I spend the next 10 minutes planning my day. I focus on identifying my TOP 1 priority—the single task that will make the biggest impact and move me closer to my biggest goals. Sometimes, my top priority may even turn into the top 3 tasks, but usually, there is always one key task that, when completed, makes other areas of my life feel easier and more aligned with my overall vision. I make sure to target this task first thing in the morning when my energy and focus are at their peak. By dedicating my early energy to this priority, I set myself up for a productive day and ensure that my efforts are focused on what matters most.

While working, I use a walking treadmill for 60-90 minutes. It's a simple way to stay active while checking off tasks. I especially use it when I'm working on repetitive tasks, like answering emails or organizing documents, that don't require my full concentration. This keeps me physically engaged, helping my mind stay focused and clear, while also allowing me to get some movement in throughout the day. It's also been shown to be a very effective routine for burning fat—studies suggest that walking can be more effective for fat burning than running, so it's a win-win for both productivity and fitness.

Every other day, I make sure to set aside time during lunch to hit the gym. Taking a break for a workout in the middle of the day gives me a chance to refresh both my mind and body, leaving me with more energy to power through the rest of the day. When you pair regular exercise with healthy eating, the benefits multiply. High-intensity workouts, along with a protein-rich diet, are a winning combination that helps me feel strong and focused. And, of course, I still enjoy the occasional trip to McDonald's with my kids—balance is key!

At the end of the day, I take a little time to reflect on what I've accomplished. I think about the things that went well and the areas where I can improve, and I make sure to appreciate the progress I've made. Then, I take a moment to jot down the top goals for the next day. This helps me feel prepared and gives me a sense of control, making it easier to wind down and rest well for tomorrow.

I make sure to spend my evenings with my family, enjoying quality time and unwinding together. Every evening, I have time to listen to an audiobook or podcast while waiting for my kids to fall asleep after our bedtime routine. I always use headphones so I can stay quiet and be present with them while they settle in. It's a peaceful, productive way to end the day.

The goal is to be in bed by 10 PM, ensuring enough sleep to recharge for the next day. Proper rest is essential for maintaining energy levels and staying productive. Life, of course, doesn't always go as planned, and things can occasionally get off track. But when that happens, the focus shifts to getting back to the routine as soon as possible. This routine is powerful, and there's a strong sense of urgency to return to it, as it helps maintain focus, boosts energy, and keeps things moving in the right direction.

The real magic starts to unfold after sticking with this routine for about a month. You'll begin to notice how much more organized and productive you feel each day. Your energy will soar, and you'll feel more in control of your time instead of being pulled in every direction. It's a simple shift, but it makes such a big difference. Take a moment to try it out, and don't worry about getting it perfect—just adjust it to fit your life. I truly believe you'll be amazed by how much better you feel as you make this small change. You've got this!

Keep Going

It's easy to give up. Anyone can do it. In fact, the world is filled with people who start something, hit a roadblock, and then walk away. But the key to winning—whether it's in business, relationships, or personal growth—isn't about avoiding tough times. It's about having the strength to push through them, to do it anyway, even when every fiber of your being wants to quit. When everything feels overwhelming, when you feel drained and out of energy, and when it seems like it would just be easier to go back to the comfort of what's familiar—that's exactly when the real test of your character happens.

The trick isn't to have more willpower than others—it's about a decision. A decision to change how you see giving up. Instead of viewing it as a relief or an escape, you have to see it for what it truly is: a choice that leads to long-term consequences. When you give up, it's not just about stopping that particular task; you're giving up your future. Every time you stop, you stop building the life you want. Every moment of quitting is a moment lost toward creating the life you dream of.

Think about this for a second: what do you lose when you give up now? Imagine waking up tomorrow, only to realize you've made no progress toward your goals. Imagine still being stuck in the same place, with the same dreams, but no closer to reaching them. What would that feel like? The stagnation, the frustration, the disappointment of realizing you've gotten nowhere. Now, ask yourself: is that really worth it? Is it really worth throwing away everything you've worked for? For me, I always remind myself that giving up means going back to a life that doesn't match my values. I think about what it would mean to fall back into that old routine, the one that keeps you just getting by, paycheck to paycheck, with no hope of getting out.

I remember the time when I felt stuck. No matter how hard I worked, it didn't seem like I was making any headway. I even considered quitting—giving up on the vision of financial freedom I had worked so hard for. I thought about stepping away from the risks, returning to the safety of the familiar. But then I thought, "What if I stop now?" If I stopped, I would be just like everyone else who didn't have the guts to keep going. I'd be back to living paycheck to paycheck, unable to do anything that made me feel free or fulfilled. And that scared me more than anything else. I couldn't accept going back to that life.

That's the key. Every time I was tempted to stop, I reminded myself of what I stood to lose. Sure, there would have been relief in quitting, but that momentary ease would have cost me everything I was working toward. The discomfort of continuing was nothing compared to the long-term regret I would've felt if I'd allowed myself to give up. The truth is, it's not about how tough things get—it's about understanding that you are building something better. You are building your future, and every difficult moment is an opportunity to keep moving forward.

The hard days will always be there. Life doesn't get easier; you just get better at handling the challenges. The key is not to avoid struggle but to accept it. It's not about trying to sidestep the hard parts of the journey; it's about learning that those moments are where growth happens. Success doesn't come from avoiding discomfort; it comes from facing it head-on and knowing that every challenge is just a stepping stone on the path toward your goals.

So, the next time you feel like giving up, remember: that the pain of pushing through will eventually fade, but the pain of giving up will stay with you for much longer. Success is not just about reaching the destination—it's about knowing that you gave it everything you had, that you stayed in the game, and that you never had to look back with regret. When you feel like quitting, ask yourself: "What will I lose if I give up right now?" The answer will be your motivation to keep going, to keep moving forward.

7

Passing on Financial Wisdom

Achieving financial freedom isn't just about benefiting yourself—it's about creating a legacy and leaving a lasting impact on those around you. One of the most rewarding parts of your financial journey is sharing the knowledge and habits that helped you succeed with others. By teaching your family, especially your children, the principles of financial independence, and by giving back to the communities and causes that matter to you, you make your success even more meaningful.

Teaching Family

Passing on financial wisdom to your family, especially your children, is one of the most impactful and valuable gifts you can give. It's about setting them up for success, ensuring they not only understand money but also develop the habits and mindset to manage it wisely throughout their lives. When you teach your children the fundamentals—how money works, how to manage it, and how to use it as a tool to achieve their goals—you provide them with the knowledge and confidence to make informed financial decisions as they grow older. These early lessons form the foundation for financial independence, empowering them to make better choices, avoid common pitfalls, and take charge of their own financial future.

The key is to start small and make learning about money fun and engaging. Begin with simple concepts like distinguishing between needs and wants. Help them understand the importance of saving, budgeting, and avoiding unnecessary debt. Children absorb these lessons best when they're given real-world examples, so take them with you when you go shopping and let them participate in the decision-making process. Show them how you stick to a budget or explain how you decide whether something is a necessity or a luxury. By involving them in practical, everyday situations, you bring these lessons to life in a way that feels relatable and memorable.

Another great way to instill financial discipline is by giving them an allowance or assigning small tasks to manage money on their own. Whether it's saving up for a desired toy or managing a small portion of their earnings, letting them experience the process of budgeting and saving gives them confidence and a sense of control over their finances. Encourage them to set their own goals, whether it's saving for something special or learning to manage a specific amount of money. The act of saving toward a goal helps build discipline and teaches them the power of delayed gratification, an invaluable skill they'll carry with them for life.

Perhaps one of the most powerful lessons you can teach is the concept of compound interest. The magic of seeing money grow exponentially over time is a lesson that can have a profound impact on their financial future. You don't need to dive into complicated formulas—simply show them how saving even a small amount regularly can lead to big rewards down the line. Using basic financial tools like savings accounts, you can demonstrate the benefits of starting early, showing them that the earlier they start saving, the greater the reward. By making the concept of compound interest easy to understand and tangible, you ignite their curiosity about money and set them on the path toward long-term financial growth.

The key is to keep things simple, start early, and build their understanding gradually. These lessons will not only help them make smarter financial choices but will also shape their relationship with money in a positive way, creating habits that will serve them throughout their lives. The greatest gift you can give them is the knowledge and confidence to create their financial success, and that starts with teaching them the basics of money from an early age.

Giving Back

rue fulfillment isn't something that can be bought, no matter how much wealth you accumulate. It doesn't come from luxury items or the accolades of success. It comes from what you give to others—the lives you touch, the help you offer, and the positive change you create. The richest moments in life often stem from the impact you make on those around you, and the greatest joy often comes from seeing the difference your actions have made in someone else's life.

As you work toward financial freedom, it's important to keep this truth in mind: your wealth is a tool. And the true power of that tool comes when you use it to uplift others. When you give, whether through your time, resources, or knowledge, you build a sense of purpose that no material possessions can provide. Giving doesn't always have to be grand gestures. Sometimes, it's the small, thoughtful actions—a kind word, a helping hand, a donation to a cause close to your heart—that make the biggest impact.

You don't have to wait until you've achieved massive financial success to start giving. Start small and let the act of giving become a habit in your life. Perhaps it's helping a friend in need, supporting a local charity, or spending time mentoring someone who could use guidance. By helping others along your journey, you begin to see the world differently. The fulfillment you find in giving is a deeper sense of satisfaction that is far more lasting than any material success.

One of the most beautiful aspects of giving is that it's not just about what you give—it's about how you make others feel. When you contribute to someone else's well-being, whether through financial support, offering your expertise, or simply listening, you create a ripple effect that spreads beyond what you may ever realize. Even the smallest gesture can spark a change in someone's life, helping them move forward in ways you can't predict.

Incorporating giving into your daily life should feel like a natural extension of who you are. You don't have to have millions to make a difference. By making giving a regular part of your journey, you show the people around you that wealth is not just something to accumulate—it's something to share. And when you pass on your knowledge of financial freedom, whether to your children, your family, or your community, you create a lasting legacy that goes far beyond what you could ever achieve on your own.

Imagine the profound impact you'll have when others are inspired by your generosity. You show them that money is not the end goal, but the means to create a positive, lasting change in the world. You teach that financial freedom is not just for personal enjoyment—it's a platform for doing good and making the world a better place. You become a beacon of hope and inspiration, encouraging others to take their steps toward financial independence while also giving back in their unique ways.

When you make giving a central part of your life, you'll find that it becomes a source of endless joy and contentment. The more you share, the more your heart fills with the deep satisfaction of knowing you've contributed to something bigger than yourself. Giving is not a sacrifice—it's an investment in the well-being of others and the creation of a legacy that will outlast any material success.

In the end, the richest life you can live is one filled with generosity, kindness, and the satisfaction that comes from knowing you've made a difference. True fulfillment lies in what we give, not what we accumulate. By sharing your wealth, time, and knowledge, you'll find a joy that far surpasses anything money can buy. And through that, you will discover the greatest wealth of all—inner peace and the deep fulfillment of having contributed to the world in a meaningful way.

8

Conclusion

As you reach the end of this book, I want to leave you with an important message: financial freedom isn't just for a "lucky few" or "special people." It's an option for anyone willing to put in the work and follow the right steps. No matter where you are starting from, you have the power to change your financial future. It won't always be easy, but it is possible.

Why should you at least consider financial freedom as a goal? Because if you don't, there's a chance it will quietly linger in your mind as *"what if?"*—a missed opportunity you can never get back. Financial freedom isn't just about having more money; it's about having more choices. It means waking up every day knowing that *you* call the shots—not your job, not your bills, and not someone else's schedule. It means being able to spend time with your family, travel the world, chase your passions, or simply enjoy peace of mind. Without it, you may always wonder what life *could have been* if you'd just taken that chance. Financial freedom gives you options, and options give you control. And once you have control, you never have to wonder *"what if?"*

again.

Remember that true success isn't just about you. It's about the impact you make on others. Real fulfillment doesn't come from buying more "stuff" — it comes from helping others. Once you reach financial freedom, consider how you can give back. Teach your children how to manage money, so they can have a better future. Share what you've learned with others, so they can improve their lives too. Give to causes and communities that are close to your heart. You'll find that no car, no house, and no luxury item will ever bring as much joy as knowing you've made a positive impact on someone else's life.

If this book helped you in any way, I would be so grateful if you shared your thoughts by leaving a review on Amazon. Your review helps others find this book, and it allows me to create even better resources for people like you. I'd love to hear your story, your success, and your thoughts on this journey. Your feedback truly matters to me.

It's just the beginning of something much bigger. The seeds of financial freedom have been planted. Now it's time to water them with action, patience, and a clear vision for your future. The life you dream of is possible. It's within reach.

9

Resources

Amram, Y., PhD. (2024, December 6). Counting blessings: The key to a healthier, happier, and more resilient you. Psychology Today. https://www.psychologytoday.com/intl/blog/spiritual-intelligence/202412/a-year-round-attitude-of-gratitude

Choosing between funds & individual securities | Vanguard. (n.d.). https://investor.vanguard.com/investor-resources-education/understanding-investment-types/choosing-between-funds-individual-securities

Folger, J. (2024, October 28). How Airbnb works—for hosts, guests, and the company itself. Investopedia. https://www.investopedia.com/articles/personal-finance/032814/pros-and-cons-using-airbnb.asp

Gilchrist, T. (2014, April 2). Wolf of Wall Street Writer on Jordan Belfort's "Quaint" Crimes and the Bernie Madoff connection. Forbes. https://www.forbes.com/sites/toddgilchrist/2014/04/01/wolf-of-wall-street-jordan-belfort-terence-w inter-bernie-madoff-quaaludes/

Loeppky, J. (2022, May 7). There's a Lot to Learn From Sports Psychology—Even if You Aren't an Athlete. Verywell Mind. https://www.verywellmind.com/how-sports-psychology-applies-outside-athletics-5226027

Stein, J. (2007, February 14). Has Jim Carrey flipped out? TIME. https://time.com/archive/6680022/has-jim-carrey-flipped-out/

Swimnerd. (n.d.). Bob Bowman | 10 Secrets of Success. The Swimnerd Newsletter. https://www.swimspam.com/p/the-10-secrets-to-success-by-bob-bowman-coach-of-michael-phelps

Tamplin, T. (2024, January 26). What does the 80/20 rule mean? | Finance Strategists. Finance Strategists. https://www.financestrategists.com/wealth-management/macroeconomics/what-does-the-80-20-rule-mean/

Team, R. D. P. F. (2015, May 7). Assets vs. Liabilities: The Difference is Life Changing. Rich Dad | Financial Education & Coaching for Everyone. https://www.richdad.com/assets-vs-liabilities

Whiteside, E. (2024, August 22). The 50/30/20 budget rule explained with examples. Investopedia. https://www.investopedia.com/ask/answers/022916/what-502030-budget-rule.asp

www.ingramcontent.com/pod-product-compliance
Lightning Source LLC
Chambersburg PA
CBHW050317230526
45471CB00005B/2226